Analysis of Truss with MSC Patran/Nastran: Tutorial and Verification

Victor Y. Perel

Copyright © 2020 by Victor Y. Perel.

All rights reserved.

ISBN: 9798640461220

Contents

Introduction 4

1 Analysis of truss by the method of joints 5

2 Patran/Nastran model 10

    2.1 Creating the model geometry 10

    2.2 Specifying material properties 14

    2.3 Specifying element properties 17

    2.4 Creating elements 21

    2.5 Applying boundary conditions 25

        2.5.1 Applying boundary conditions at joint A 25

        2.5.2 Applying boundary conditions at joint B 34

        2.5.3 Applying boundary conditions at joint C 38

    2.6 Applying loads 42

    2.7 Running Analysis 47

    2.8 Viewing results of analysis 52

        2.8.1 Viewing internal forces in rods 52

        2.8.2 Viewing components of stress tensor 57

        2.8.3 Viewing constraint forces 59

Introduction

This text is a tutorial on using the MSC Nastran finite element analysis program with MSC Patran graphical user interface for stress analysis of a truss (Figure 1), i.e. a structure made of pin-jointed rods and loaded at the joints. The rods of a truss are deformed only in their longitudinal directions, i.e. in tension and compression.

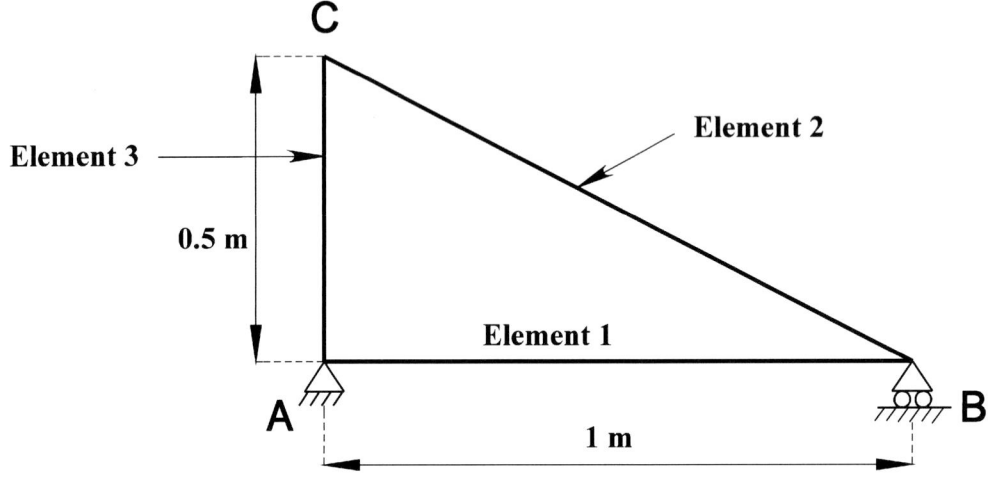

Figure 1

In the section 1 of the text, the forces and stresses in the truss members and the forces of reactions of constraints are calculated analytically by the method of joints. The section 2 of the text gives detailed instructions on solving the same problem with the use of MSC Patran/Nastran. The results of the Nastran analysis are shown to be the same as the results obtained analytically.

1 Analysis of truss by the method of joints

We are considering the truss in Figure 1, with the joint A constrained with a frictionless pin, with the joint B constrained with a roller, and with the joint C loaded by a horizontal force P=2 N. Each rod's area of cross-section is equal to $S = 0.001 m^2$.

We are solving the problem of calculating the reaction forces of the constraints and the forces and stresses in the truss members (rods). The solution of this problem by the method of joints is presented below.

Statement that the sum of force vectors, applied to the joint A, is equal to zero:

$$\vec{R}^A + \vec{F}^{AC} + \vec{F}^{AB} = \vec{0} \tag{1}$$

where $\vec{F}^{AC}$ is force applied to the joint A from the member AC;
$\vec{F}^{AB}$ is force applied to the joint A from the member AB;
$\vec{R}^A$ is reaction force applied to the joint A from its support.
In the following equations, the notations are similar.

Eq. (1) in terms of components of forces:

$$R_x^A + \underbrace{F_x^{AC}}_{0} + F_x^{AB} = 0 \tag{2}$$

$$R_y^A + F_y^{AC} + \underbrace{F_y^{AB}}_{0} = 0 \tag{3}$$

Statement that the sum of force vectors, applied to the joint B, is equal to zero:

$$\vec{R}^B + \vec{F}^{BA} + \vec{F}^{BC} = \vec{0} \tag{4}$$

Eq. (4) in terms of components of forces:

$$\underbrace{R_x^B}_{0} + F_x^{BA} + F_x^{BC} = 0 \tag{5}$$

$$R_y^B + \underbrace{F_y^{BA}}_{0} + F_y^{BC} = 0 \tag{6}$$

Statement that the sum of force vectors, applied to the joint C, is equal to zero:

$$\vec{P}+\vec{F}^{CA}+\vec{F}^{CB}=\vec{0} \tag{7}$$

Eq. (7) in terms of components of forces:

$$\underbrace{P_x}_{2}+\underbrace{F_x^{CA}}_{0}+F_x^{CB}=0 \tag{8}$$

$$\underbrace{P_y}_{0}+F_y^{CA}+F_y^{CB}=0 \tag{9}$$

Statement that the sum of external force vectors is equal to zero (force equilibrium equation of entire truss):

$$\vec{P}+\vec{R}^{A}+\vec{R}^{B}=\vec{0} \tag{10}$$

Eq. (10) in terms of components of forces:

$$\underbrace{P_x}_{2}+R_x^{A}+\underbrace{R_x^{B}}_{0}=0 \tag{11}$$

$$\underbrace{P_y}_{0}+R_y^{A}+R_y^{B}=0 \tag{12}$$

Statement of equality to zero of the sum of moments of external forces about the axis that passes through the point A and is parallel to the z-axis (moment equilibrium equation of entire truss):

$$0=\hat{e}_z\cdot\left(\overrightarrow{AC}\times\vec{P}\right)+\hat{e}_z\cdot\left(\overrightarrow{AB}\times\vec{R}^{B}\right)$$

$$=\begin{vmatrix} 0 & 0 & 1 \\ 0 & 0.5 & 0 \\ P_x & \underbrace{P_y}_{0} & \underbrace{P_z}_{0} \end{vmatrix}+\begin{vmatrix} 0 & 0 & 1 \\ 1 & 0 & 0 \\ \underbrace{R_x^{B}}_{0} & R_y^{B} & \underbrace{R_z^{B}}_{0} \end{vmatrix}=-0.5P_x+R_y^{B}$$

So, the moment equilibrium equation of the entire truss is

$$R_y^{B}-0.5\underbrace{P_x}_{2}=0 \tag{13}$$

6

Besides, we have the relations:

$$\frac{F_y^{BC}}{F_x^{BC}} = -0.5 \qquad (14)$$

and

$$\frac{F_y^{CB}}{F_x^{CB}} = -0.5 \qquad (15)$$

Let us write again all the equations involving components of forces:

$$R_x^A + \underbrace{F_x^{AC}}_{0} + F_x^{AB} = 0 \qquad \text{(eq. 2)}$$

$$R_y^A + F_y^{AC} + \underbrace{F_y^{AB}}_{0} = 0 \qquad \text{(eq. 3)}$$

$$\underbrace{R_x^B}_{0} + F_x^{BA} + F_x^{BC} = 0 \qquad \text{(eq. 5)}$$

$$R_y^B + \underbrace{F_y^{BA}}_{0} + F_y^{BC} = 0 \qquad \text{(eq. 6)}$$

$$\underbrace{P_x}_{2} + \underbrace{F_x^{CA}}_{0} + F_x^{CB} = 0 \qquad \text{(eq. 8)}$$

$$\underbrace{P_y}_{0} + F_y^{CA} + F_y^{CB} = 0 \qquad \text{(eq. 9)}$$

$$\underbrace{P_x}_{2} + R_x^A + \underbrace{R_x^B}_{0} = 0 \qquad \text{(eq. 11)}$$

$$\underbrace{P_y}_{0} + R_y^A + R_y^B = 0 \qquad \text{(eq. 12)}$$

$$R_y^B - 0.5 \underbrace{P_x}_{2} = 0 \qquad \text{(eq. 13)}$$

7

$$\frac{F_y^{BC}}{F_x^{BC}} = \frac{1}{2} \qquad \text{(eq. 14)}$$

$$\frac{F_y^{CB}}{F_x^{CB}} = \frac{1}{2} \qquad \text{(eq. 15)}$$

These are 11 equations with 11 unknowns: R_x^A, R_y^A, R_y^B, F_x^{AB}, F_x^{BA}, F_y^{AC}, F_x^{BC}, F_y^{BC}, F_x^{CB}, F_y^{CB}, F_y^{CA}. The solution of these equations is

$$R_x^A = -2, \quad R_y^A = -1, \quad R_y^B = 1 \tag{16}$$

$$-F_x^{BC} = F_x^{CB} = -2 \tag{17}$$

$$F_y^{BC} = -F_y^{CB} = -1 \tag{18}$$

$$F_y^{AC} = -F_y^{CA} = 1 \tag{19}$$

$$F_x^{AB} = -F_x^{BA} = 2 \tag{20}$$

So, components of forces, applied to the joint *A*, are

$$R_x^A = -2, \; F_x^{AB} = 2$$

$$R_y^A = -1, \; F_y^{AC} = 1$$

Components of forces, applied to the joint *B*, are

$$F_x^{BA} = -2, \; F_x^{BC} = 2$$

$$R_y^B = 1, \; F_y^{BC} = -1$$

Components of forces, applied to the joint *C*, are

$$F_x^{CB} = -2, \; P_x = 2$$

$$F_y^{CB} = 1, \; F_y^{CA} = -1$$

The forces

$$\vec{F}^{AB} = F_x^{AB} \hat{e}_x = 2\hat{e}_x \text{ and } \vec{F}^{BA} = F_x^{BA} \hat{e}_x = -2\hat{e}_x \qquad (21)$$

applied by the rod *AB* to its adjacent joints *A* and *B*, are directed toward the rod *AB*, so the rod *AB* is in tension; therefore the rod's internal force N^{AB} is positive, according to the general convention, and is equal to

$$N^{AB} = |F_x^{AB}| = |F_x^{BA}| = 2 \qquad (22)$$

The stress σ^{AB} in the rod *AB*, normal to the rod's cross-section, is

$$\sigma^{AB} = \frac{N^{AB}}{S} = \frac{2}{0.001} \frac{N}{m^2} = 2000\, Pa \qquad (23)$$

The forces

$$\vec{F}^{BC} = F_x^{BC} \hat{e}_x + F_y^{BC} \hat{e}_y = 2\hat{e}_x - \hat{e}_y$$

and

$$\vec{F}^{CB} = F_x^{CB} \hat{e}_x + F_y^{CB} \hat{e}_y = -2\hat{e}_x + \hat{e}_y$$

applied by the rod *BC* to its adjacent joints *B* and *C*, are directed away from the rod *BC*, so the rod *BC* is in compression; therefore its internal force N^{BC} is negative, according to the general convention, and is equal to

$$\begin{aligned} N^{BC} &= -\sqrt{\left(F_x^{BC}\right)^2 + \left(F_y^{BC}\right)^2} = -\sqrt{\left(F_x^{CB}\right)^2 + \left(F_y^{CB}\right)^2} \\ &= -\sqrt{2^2 + 1^2} = -2.2361 \end{aligned} \qquad (24)$$

The stress σ^{BC} in the rod *BC*, normal to the rod's cross-section, is

$$\sigma^{BC} = \frac{N^{BC}}{S} = \frac{-2.2361}{0.001} \frac{N}{m^2} = -2236.1\, Pa \qquad (25)$$

Similarly, we find that the rod *AC* is in tension, so its internal force N^{AC} is positive, and is equal to

$$N^{AC} = |F_y^{AC}| = |F_y^{CA}| = 1 \qquad (26)$$

The stress σ^{AC} in the rod *AC*, normal to the rod's cross-section, is

$$\sigma^{AC} = \frac{N^{AC}}{S} = \frac{1}{0.001}\frac{N}{m^2} = 1000\,Pa \tag{27}$$

2 Patran/Nastran model

2.1 Creating the model geometry

1) Create a new database file *truss.db*.

2) Specify display parameters of labels of points and curves.

In the main menu click **Display**;

in the drop-down menu, select **Entity Color/Label/Render…** :

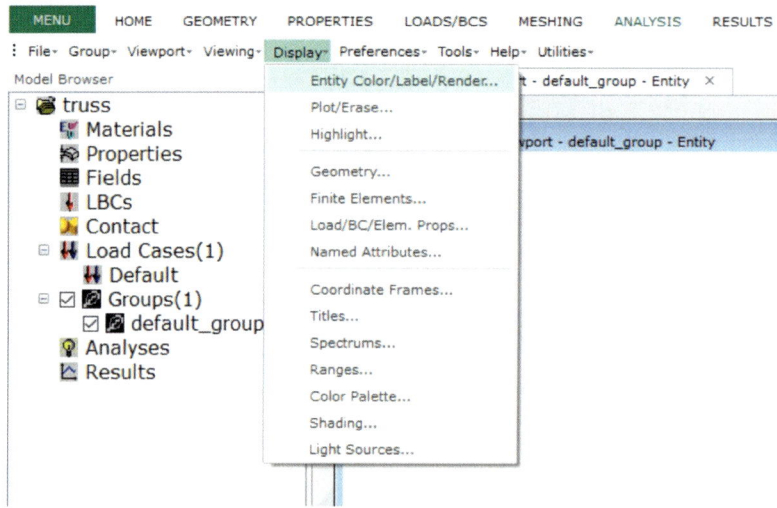

This will open the **Entity Color/Label/Render** RHS Window, where we check **Label** of **Point**, set the color of points to red, set the **Label Font Size** to 14, and click **Apply**:

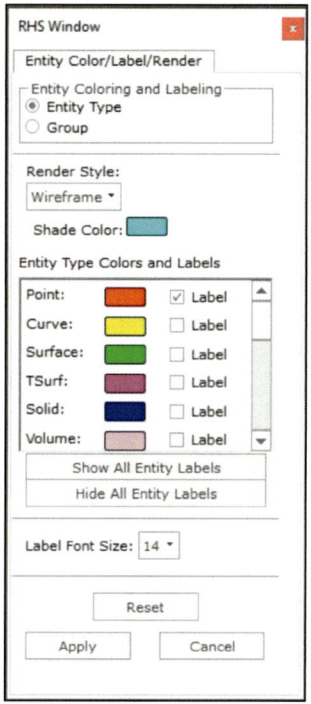

Click **Cancel** to close this panel.

In the main menu click **Display**;

in the drop-down menu, click **Geometry…**:

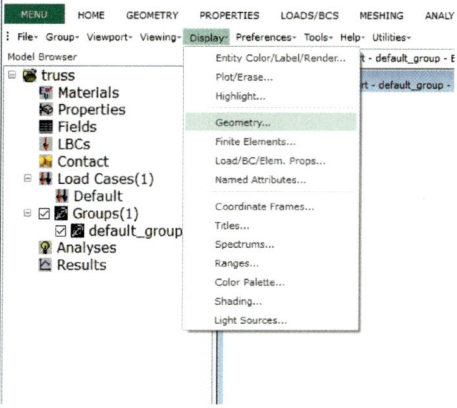

This will open the **Geometric Attributes** RHS Window, where we set **Point Size** to 10, using the slider:

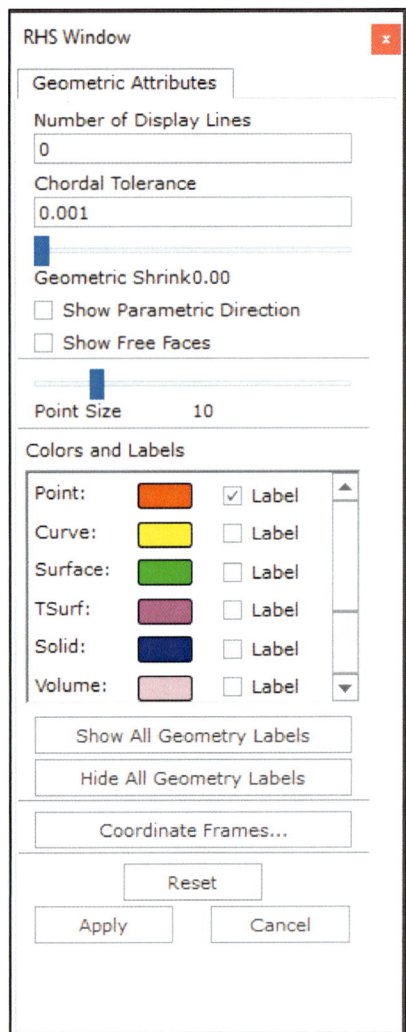

Click **Apply** and **Cancel**.

3) Create points, which represent joints of the truss.

　　Open the **GEOMETRY** application

The **Geometry** RHS Window shows up. The point ID in the **Point ID List** is set to 1 by default. Uncheck **Auto Execute**. Enter coordinates [0 0 0] of the first point, at the location the first joint of the truss:

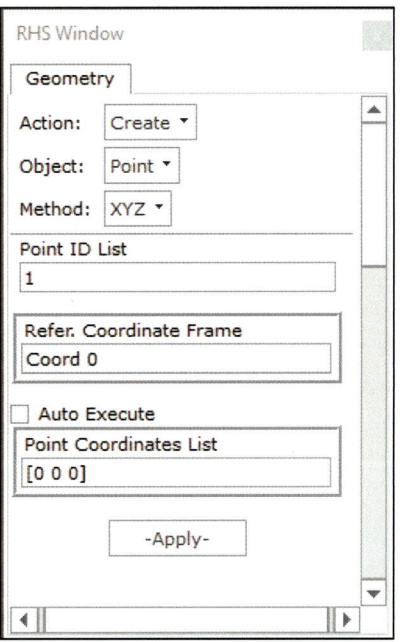

Click **Apply**. The point and its label (point ID) appear in the display window. The point ID in the **Point ID List** changes automatically from 1 to 2.

Similarly, create points with coordinates [1 0 0] and [0 0.5 0]:

Close the **Geometry** RHS Window.

2.2 Specifying material properties

Move the cursor to the model browser, right-click the mouse, in the drop-down menu select **Create ▶ Material**:

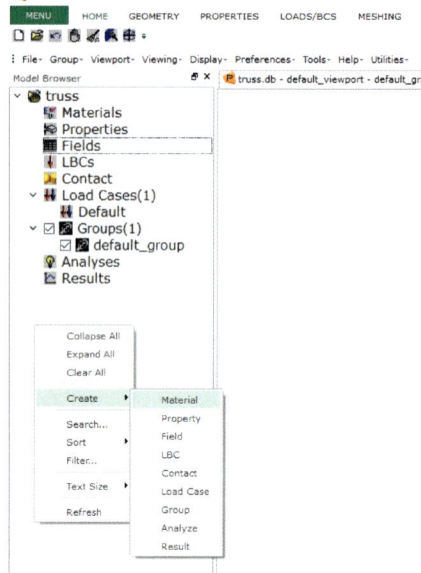

The **Materials** RHS Window shows up:

In the main menu click **Utilities**, in the drop-down menu select

Materials → Material Session File Library…

In the **Materials Library** RHS Window select *steel_iso_SI*, click **Apply**. The material name *steel_iso_SI* shows up in the **Materials** RHS Window, under **Existing Materials**:

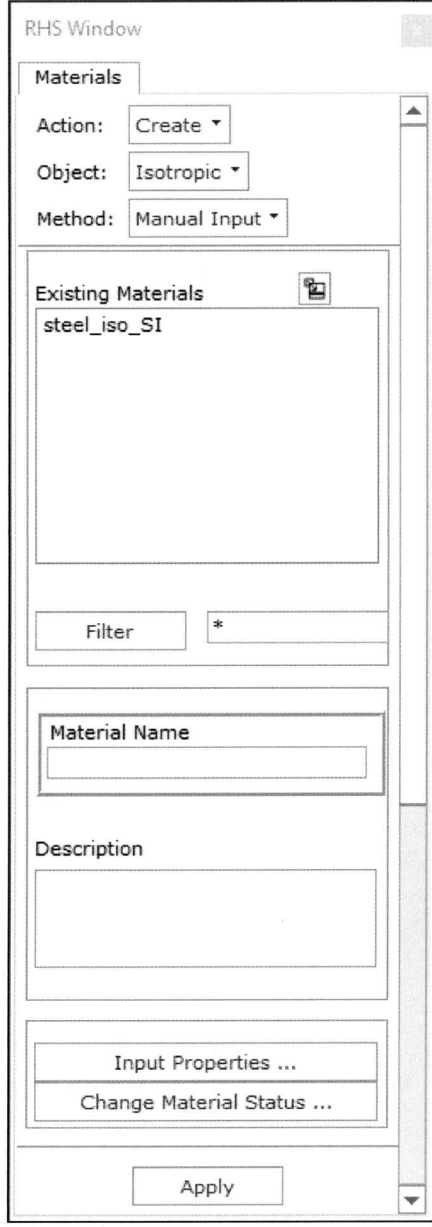

To see or edit the properties of the selected material, click the name *steel_iso_SI* in the **Materials** RHS Window, under **Existing Materials**.

15

The **Input Options** panel shows up with the editable material properties:

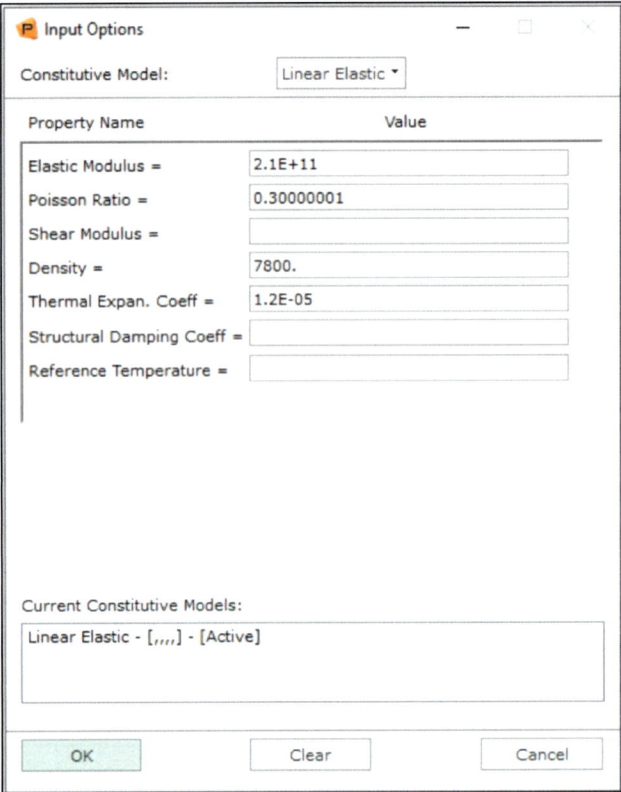

Edit the material properties, if necessary, then Click **OK** in the **Input Options** panel and click **Apply** in the RHS Window. The material name *steel_iso_SI* shows up in the **Model Browser**:

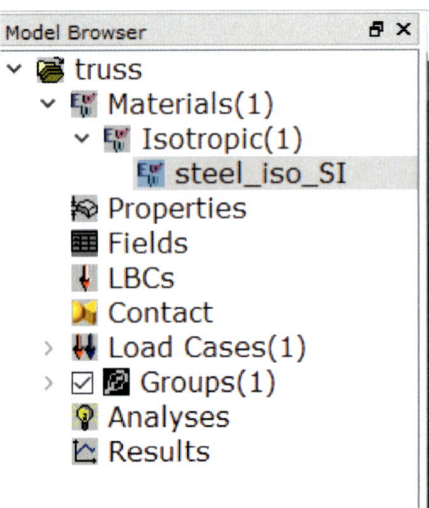

Close **Materials** RHS Window.

2.3 Specifying element properties

Open the **PROPERTIES** application:

The **Element Properties** RHS Window shows up, where we specify the following commands:

Click **Input Properties …**

The **Input Properties** panel shows up:

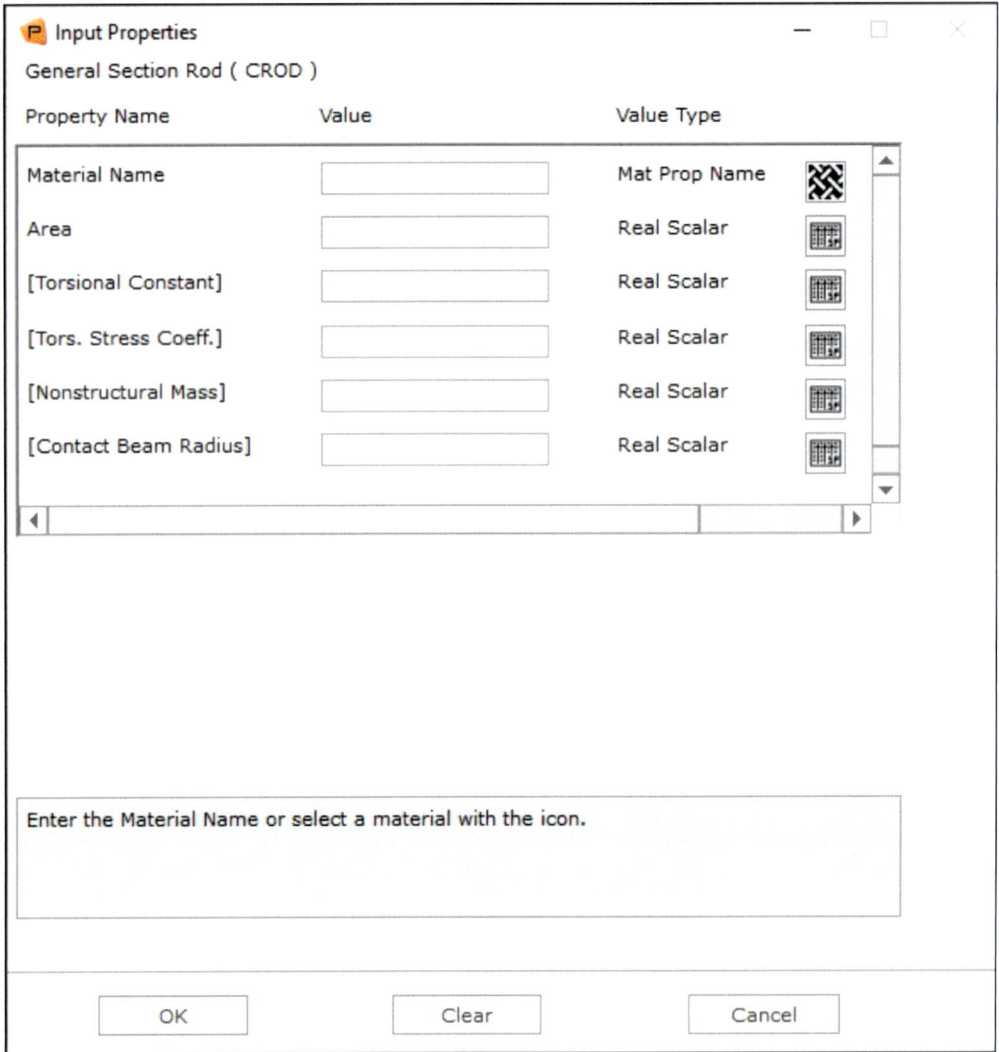

Click the **Mat Prop Name** 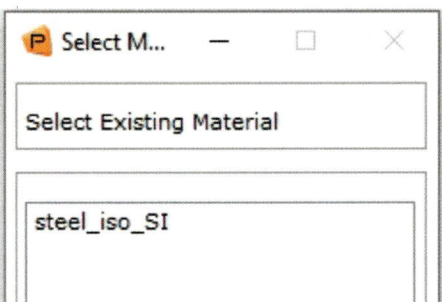, the **Select Materials** window shows up,

where we click the material name *steel_iso_SI* under **Select Existing Material**. The material name *steel_iso_SI* shows up in the **Material Name** field of the **Input Properties** panel. Set **Area** of cross-section equal to 0.001:

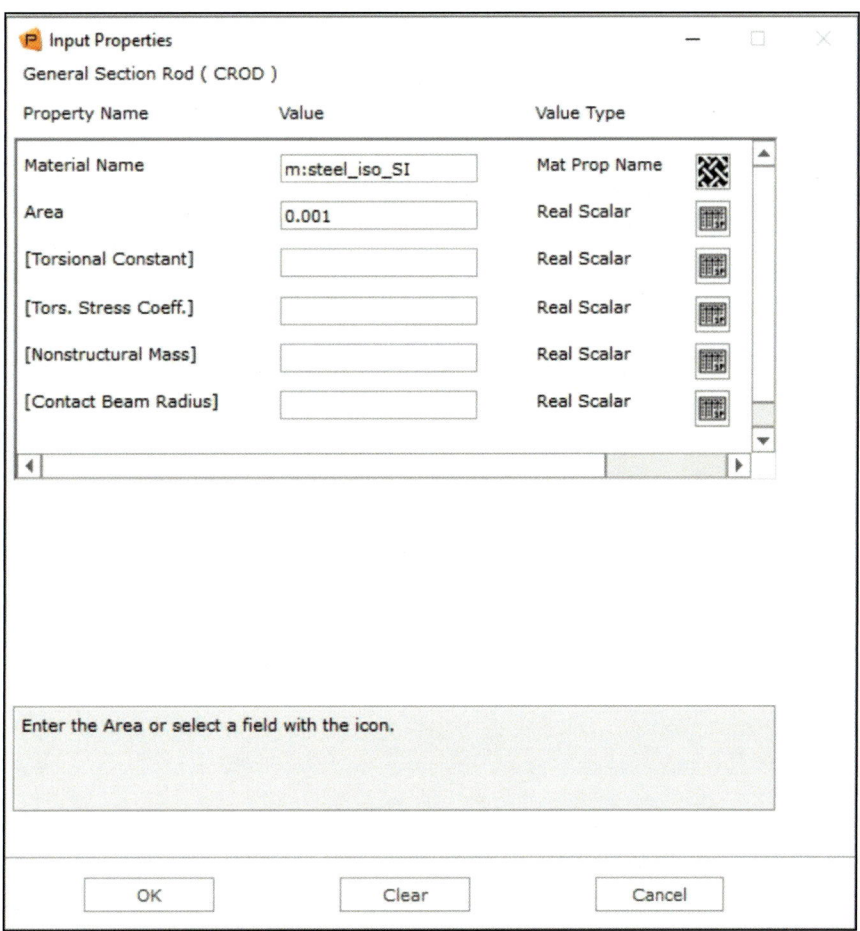

Click **OK** in the **Input Properties** panel and click **Apply** in the **Element Properties** RHS Window.

The element property name *rod_elem_prop* shows up in the **Element Properties** RHS Window in the field **Sets By: Name**

and in the **Model Browser**:

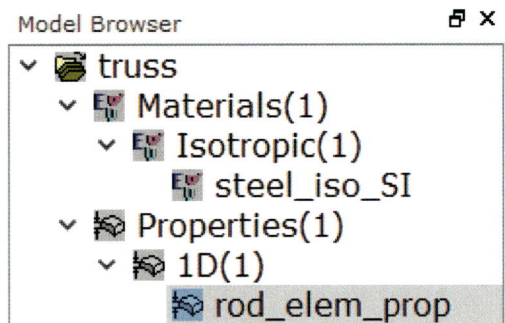

Close the **Element Properties** RHS Window.

2.4 Creating elements

Click **Display** in the main menu. In the drop-down menu select **Finite Elements…**

The **FEM Attributes** RHS Window shows up, where we set **Node Size** to 10, check **Label** of **Node**, check **Label** of **Bar**, set the color of **Node** and **Bar** to blue, and click **Apply**:

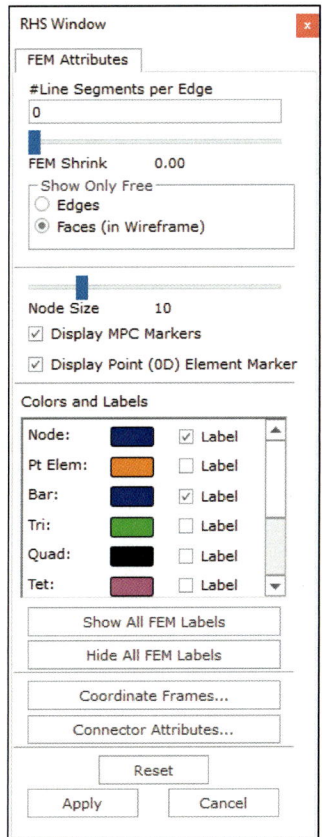

Click **Cancel** to close the RHS Window.

21

Open the **MESHING** application:

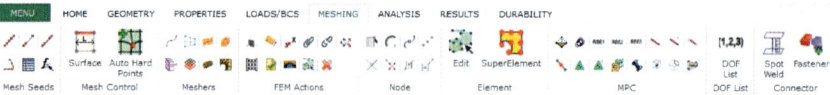

The **Finite Elements** RHS Window shows up, where we specify the following commands and uncheck **Auto Execute**:

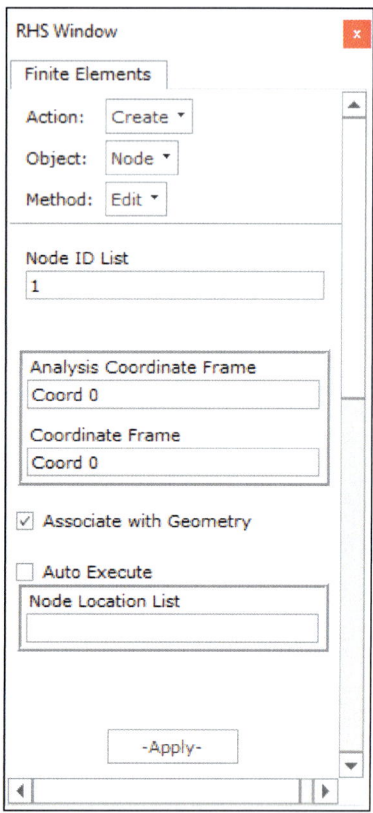

Click in the field **Node Location List**, click at Point 1 in the display window, click **Apply**. The first node and its label, **1**, show up in the display window. In the **Node ID list**, the number of the next node to be created changes automatically to **2**.

Click in the field **Node Location List**, click at Point 2 in the display window, click **Apply**. The second node and its label, **2**, show up in the display window.

Similarly, create the third node.

In the **Finite Elements** RHS Window, change **Object** to **Element**, select **Shape** as **Bar**, select **Topology** as **Bar2**, uncheck **Auto Execute**:

Click **Select Existing Prop…**

The **Property Set** panel shows up, where we select the name *rod_elem_prop* of the property set for the element that we want to create:

In the **Finite Elements** RHS Window, the element's **Prop. Name** *rod_elem_prop* shows up:

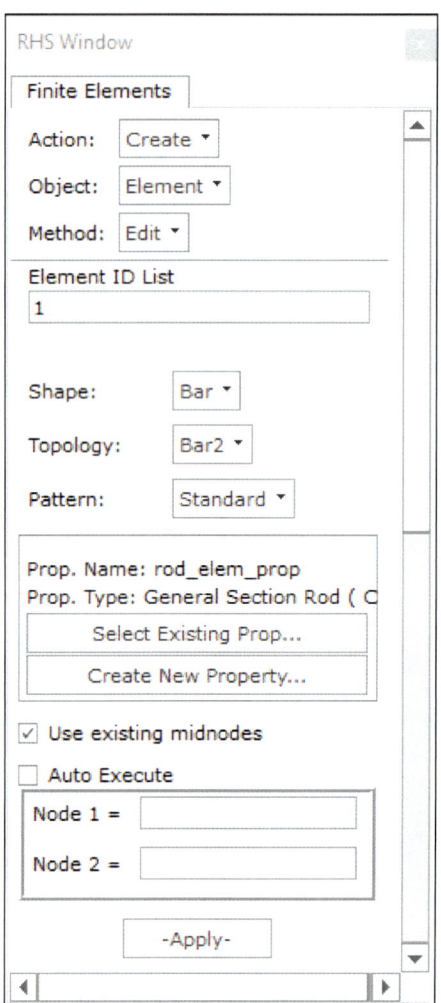

In the **Finite Elements** RHS Window, click in the **Node 1** field, then click the node with label 1 in the display window. In the **Finite Elements** RHS Window, click in the **Node 2** field, then click the node with label 2 in the display window. Click **Apply**. The first element and its label, **1**, show up in the display window. In the **Element ID List**, the number of the next element to be created changes automatically to **2**. Create the second and the third elements similarly to the first element.

The elements and their labels will look in the display window as follows:

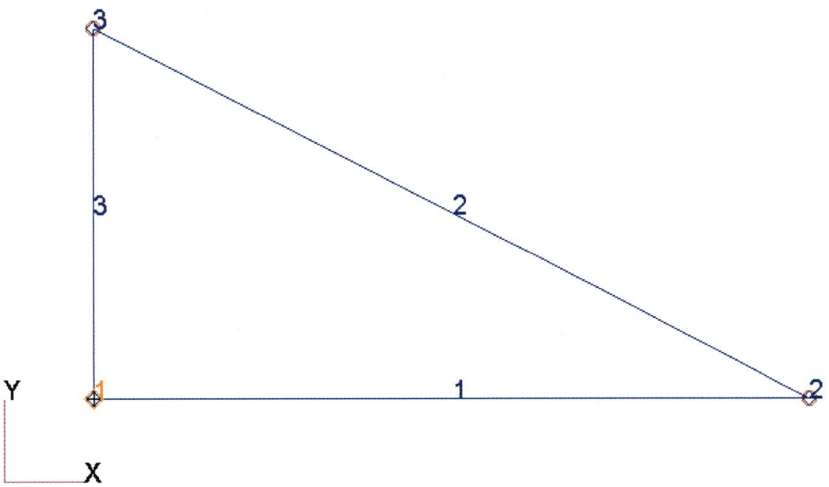

Close the **Finite Elements** RHS Window.

2.5 Applying boundary conditions

2.5.1 Applying boundary conditions at joint A

In the main menu click **Display**, in the drop-down menu select **Load/BC/Elem. Props…**

This will open **LBC/Elem. Prop. Attributes** RHS Window, where we make sure that the **Displacement** and **Force**, under **Loads/BCs,** are checked, and set the color of **Displacement** and **Force** to red. Click **Apply**.

Click **Label Style…**

The **Label Style** RHS Window shows up, in which we set **Label Format: Fixed**, and set number of **Significant figures** to 2:

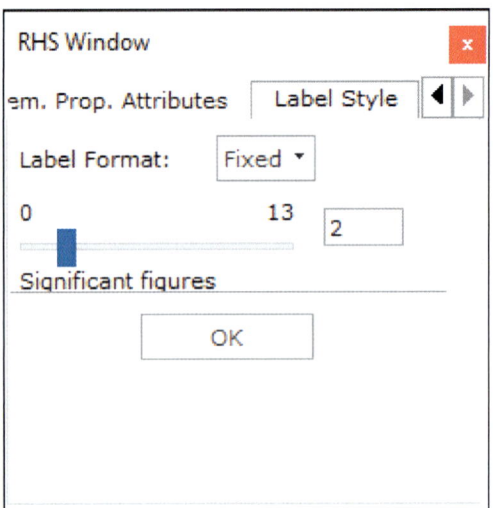

Click **OK** in the **Label Style** RHS Window. Click **Cancel** in the RHS Window. Close the **Finite Elements** RHS Window.

Open the **LOADS/BCS** application:

The **Load/Boundary Conditions** RHS Window shows up, where we specify the commands and the **New Set Name** *BC1* to create the boundary conditions at the joint *A* (node 1):

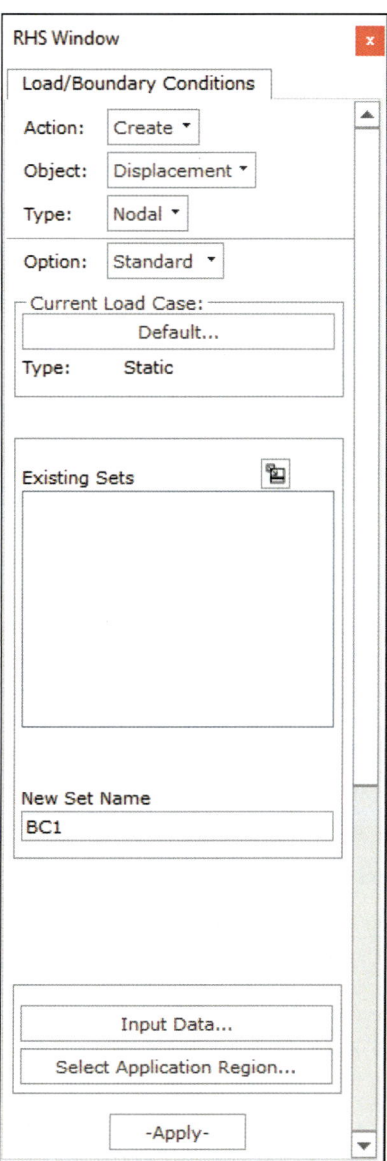

Click **Input Data…**

The **Input Data** panel shows up, where we impose constraints on nodal variables:

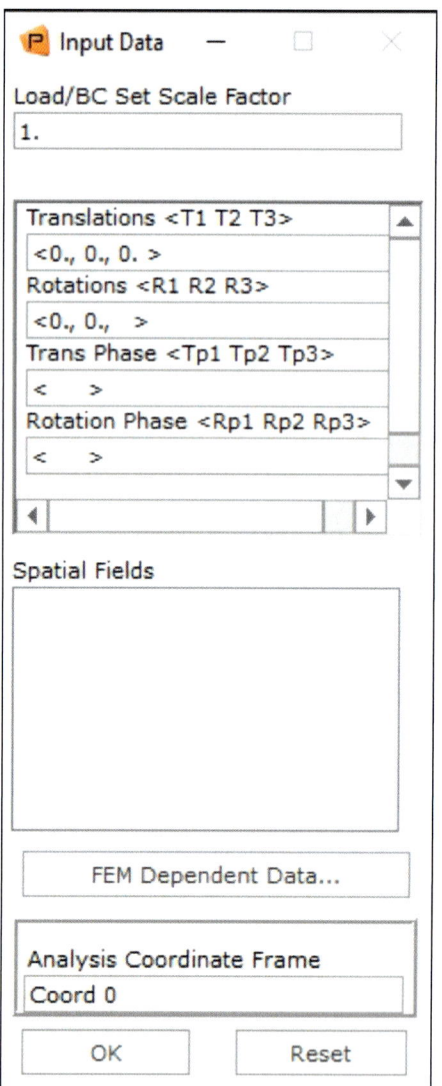

Click **OK** in the **Input Data** panel.

Click **Select Application Region…** in the **Load/Boundary Conditions** RHS Window, the **Select Application Region** RHS Window shows up, where we specify the command **Select: FEM**

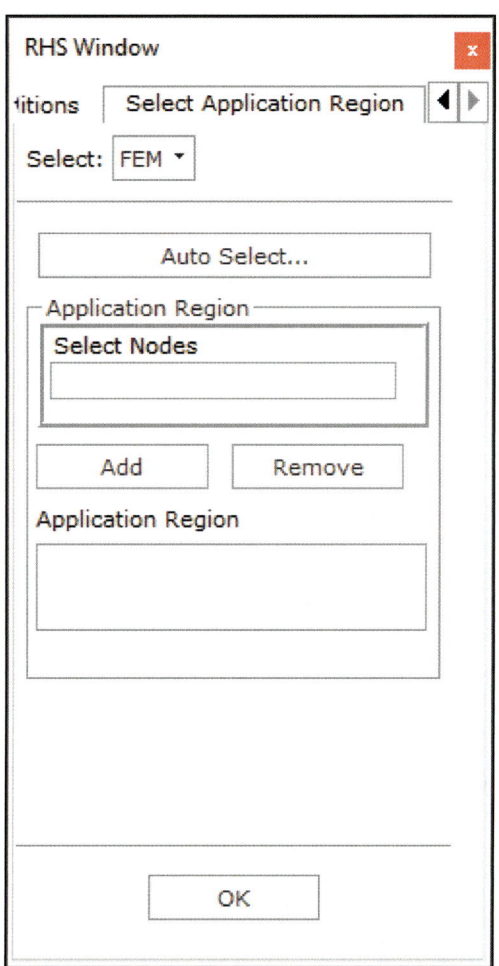

Click in the **Select Nodes** field, click at the Node 1 in the display window,

Node 1 shows up in the **Select Nodes** field:

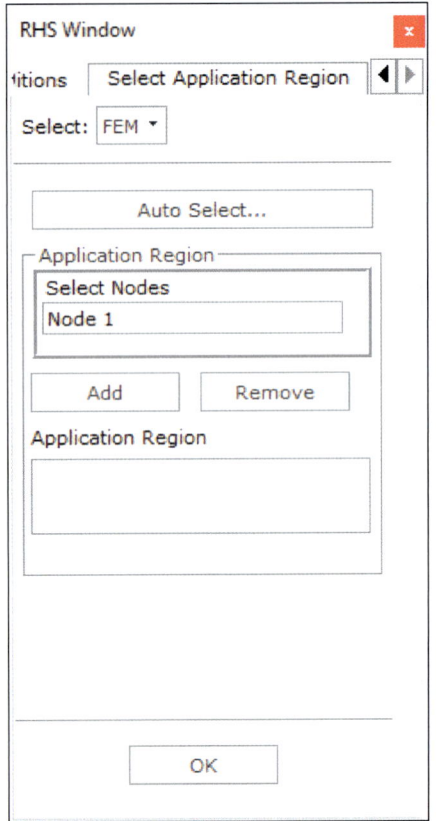

In the **Select Application Region** RHS Window, click **Add**, the **Node 1** name moves into the **Application Region** field:

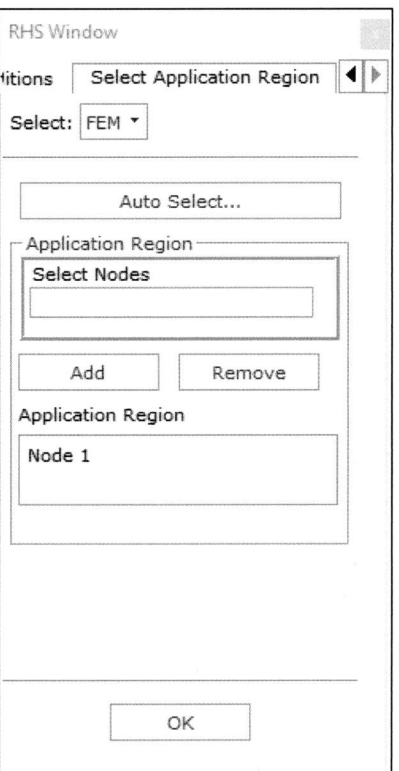

Click **OK**.

In the **Load/Boundary Conditions** RHS Window, click **Apply**. The name *BC1* moves into the **Existing Sets** field:

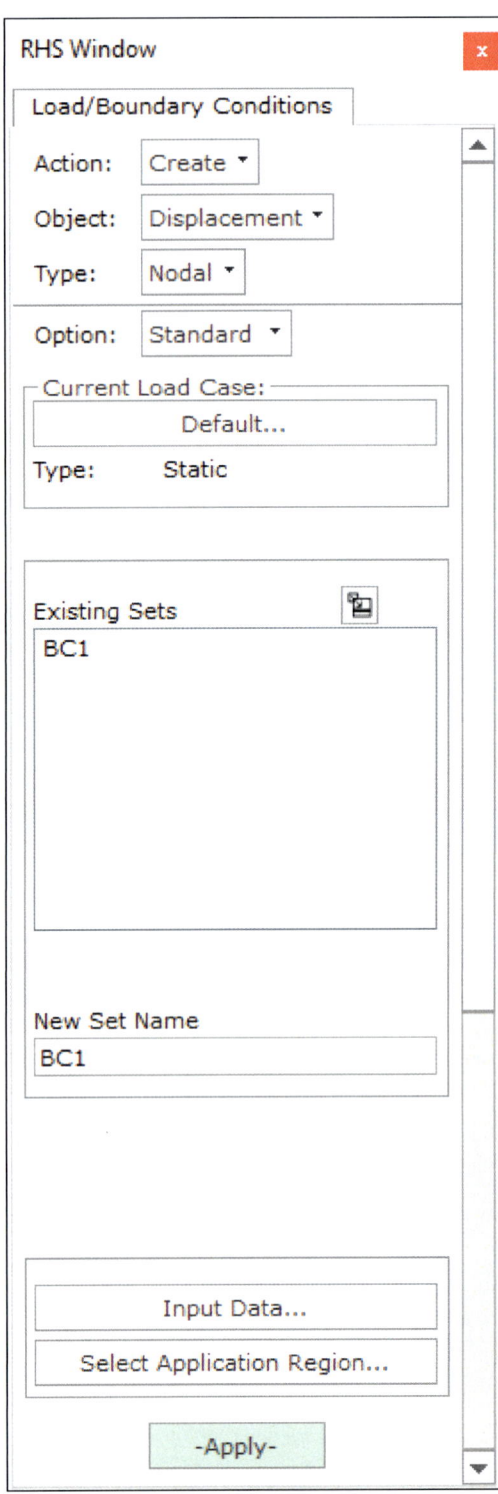

and the name *BC1* shows up in the **Model Browser**:

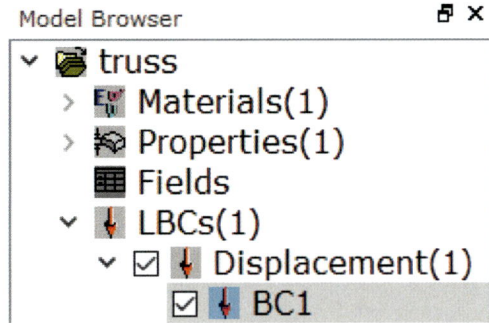

Numbers **12345** of the constrained nodal variables show up near the Node 1 in the display window:

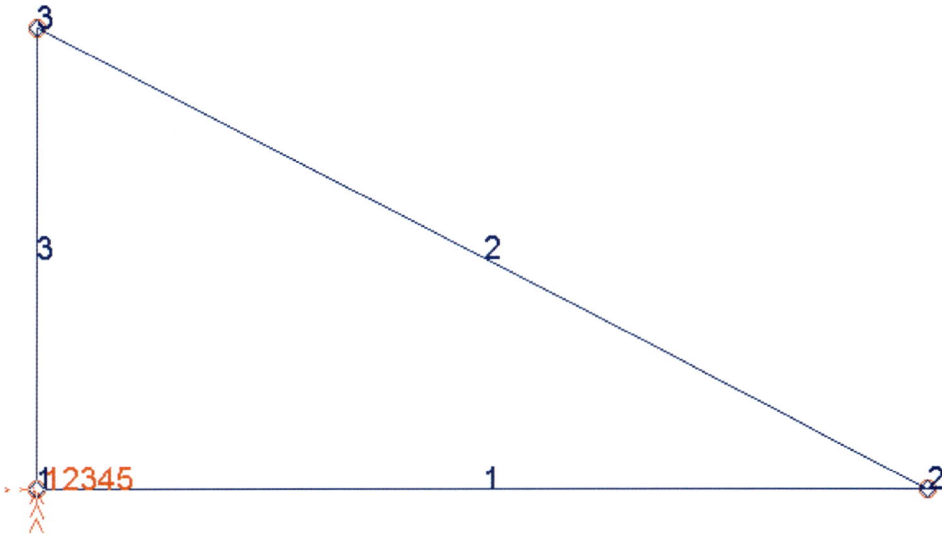

2.5.2 Applying boundary conditions at joint B

In the field **New Set Name**, type *BC2*. Click **Input Data…**

The panel **Input Data** shows up, where we impose constraints on nodal variables of the joint *B* (Node 2):

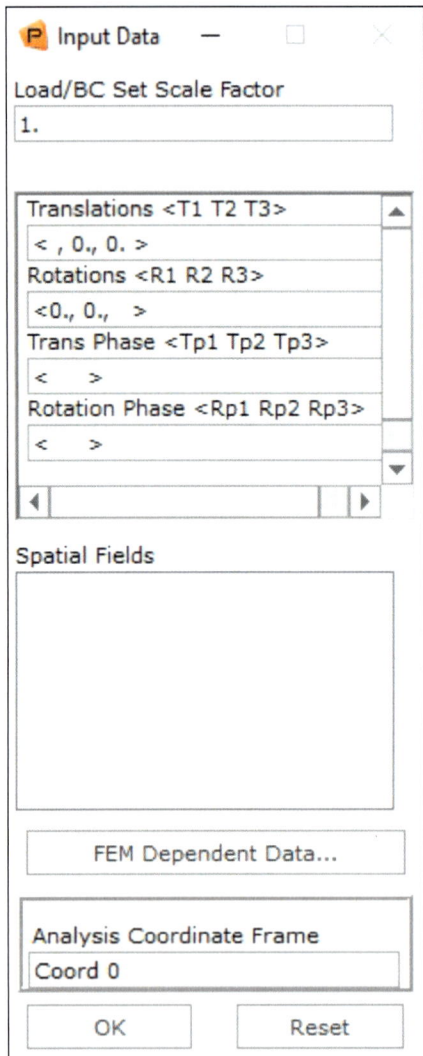

Click **OK** in the panel **Input Data**.

In the RHS Window **Load/Boundary Conditions**, click **Select Application Region…**

The panel **Select Application Region** shows up, where we click in the field **Select Nodes** and click the Node 2 in the display window, the name **Node 2** shows up in the **Select Nodes** field:

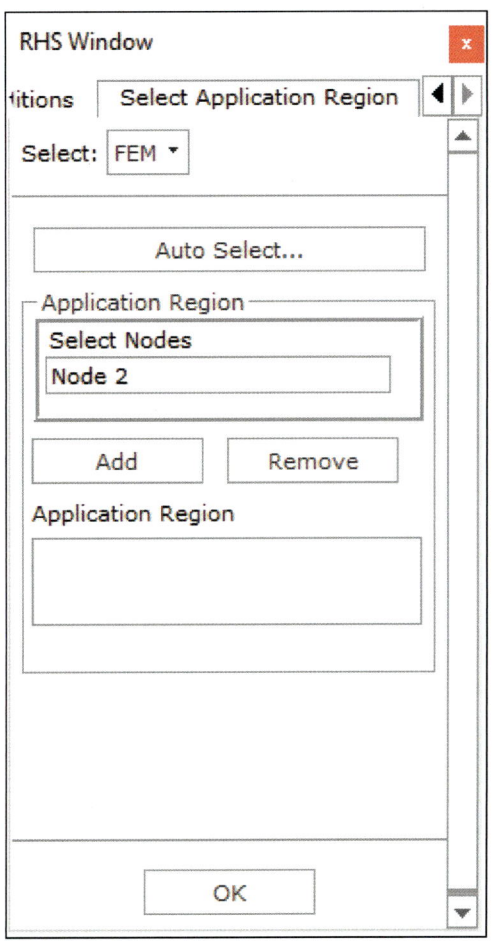

In the **Select Application Region** RHS Window, click **Add and OK**.

In the **Load/Boundary Conditions** RHS Window, click **Apply**.

The name *BC2* moves into the field **Existing Sets**:

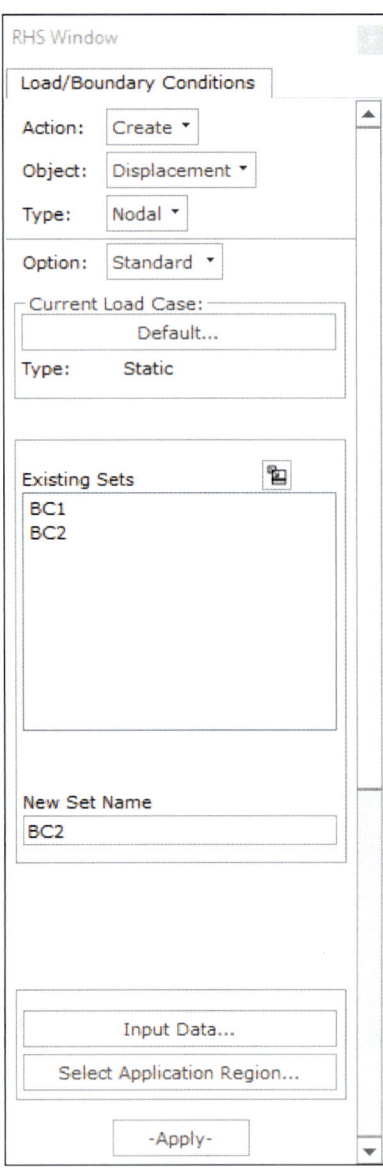

and the name *BC2* shows up in the **Model Browser**:

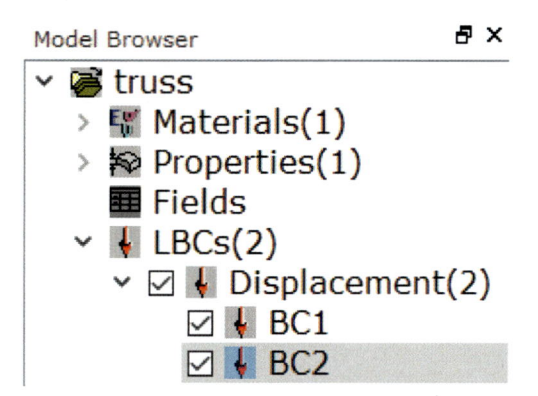

Numbers **2345** of the constrained nodal variables show up near the Node 2 in the display window:

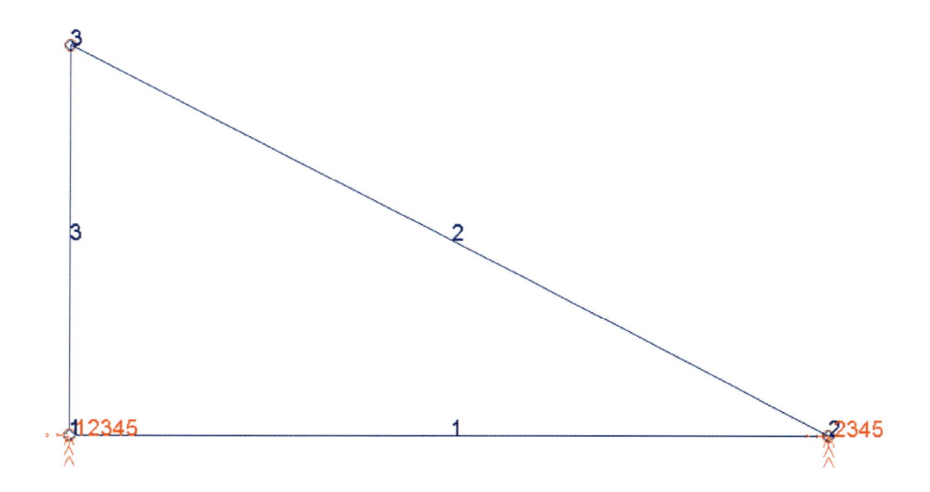

2.5.3 Applying boundary conditions at joint C

In the field **New Set Name**, type *BC3*. Click **Input Data…**

The panel **Input Data** shows up, where we impose constraints on nodal variables of the joint *C* (Node 3):

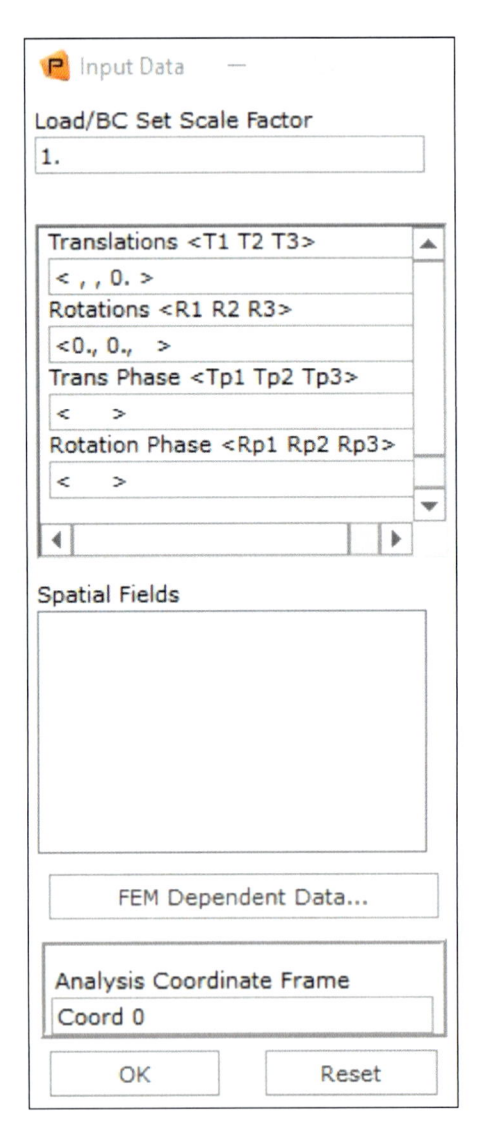

```
Input Data

Load/BC Set Scale Factor
1.

Translations <T1 T2 T3>
< , , 0. >
Rotations <R1 R2 R3>
<0., 0., >
Trans Phase <Tp1 Tp2 Tp3>
<     >
Rotation Phase <Rp1 Rp2 Rp3>
<     >

Spatial Fields


FEM Dependent Data…

Analysis Coordinate Frame
Coord 0

     OK            Reset
```

Click **OK** in the panel **Input Data**.

In the **Load/Boundary Conditions** RHS Window, click **Select Application Region…**

The panel **Select Application Region** shows up, where we click in the field **Select Nodes** and click the Node 3 in the display window, the name **Node 3** shows up in the field **Select Nodes**:

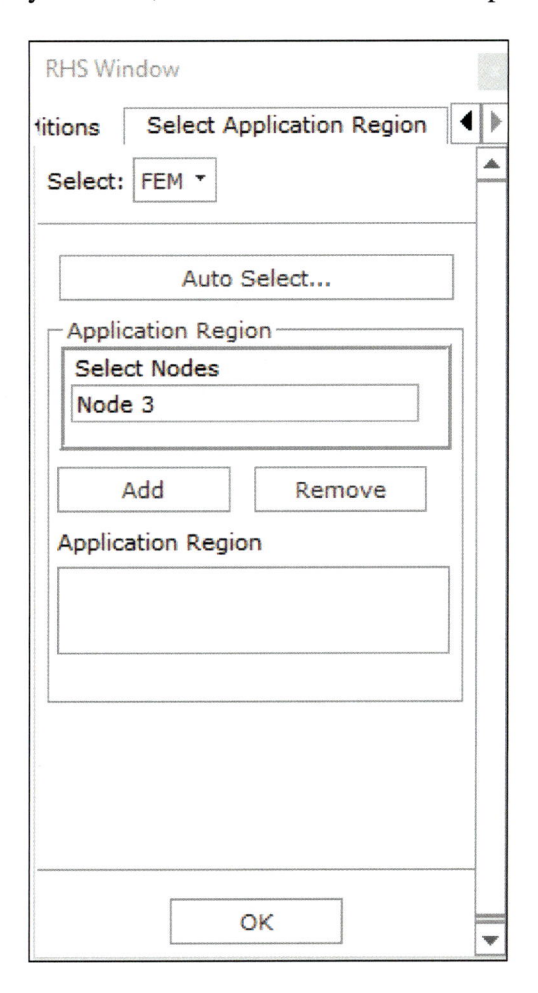

In the **Select Application Region** RHS Window, click **Add and OK**.

In the RHS Window **Load/Boundary Conditions**, click **Apply**. The name *BC3* moves into the field **Existing Sets**:

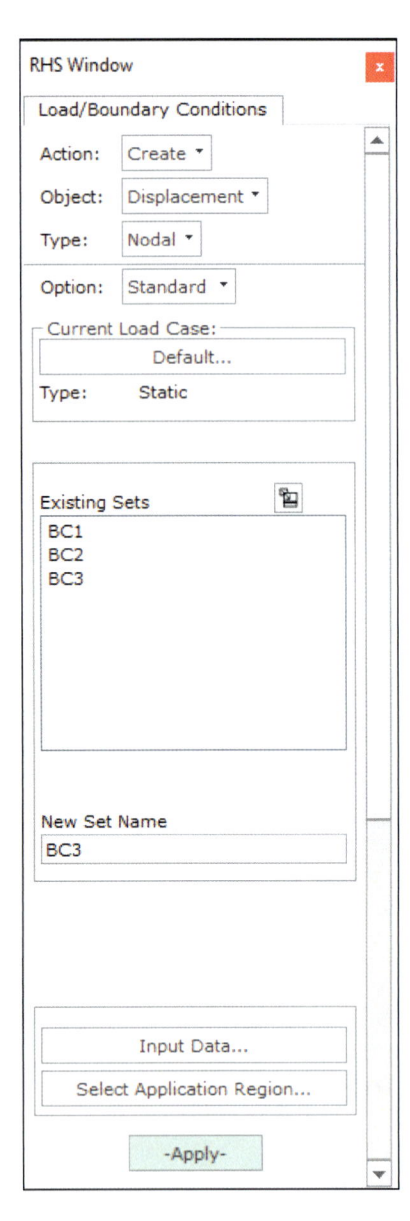

and the name *BC3* shows up in the **Model Browser**:

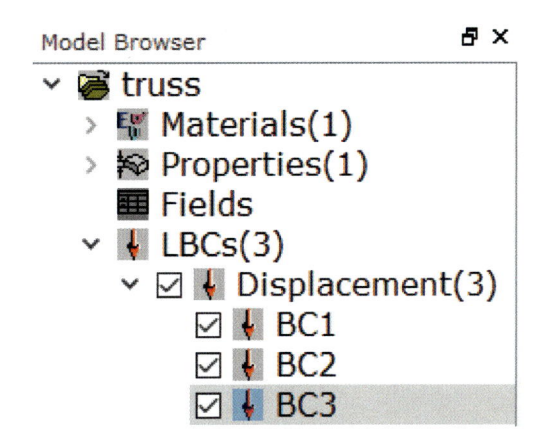

Numbers 345 of the constrained nodal variables show up near the Node 3 in the display window:

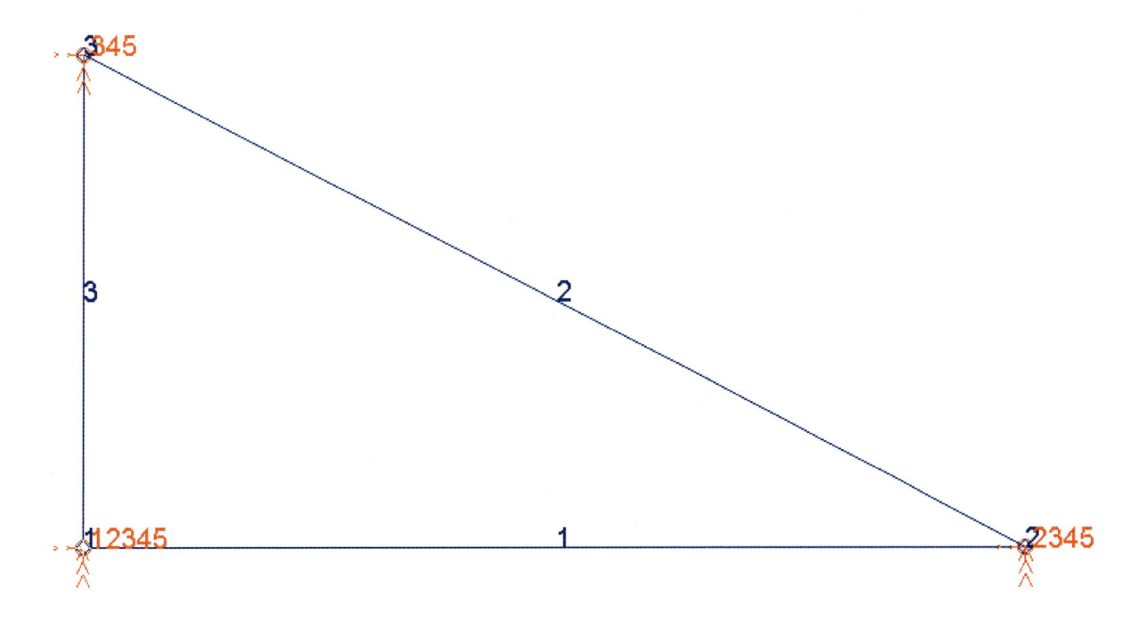

2.6 Applying loads

In the **Load/Boundary Conditions** RHS Window, specify the following commands:

Click **Input Data…**

The **Input Data** panel shows up, where we specify components of the force:

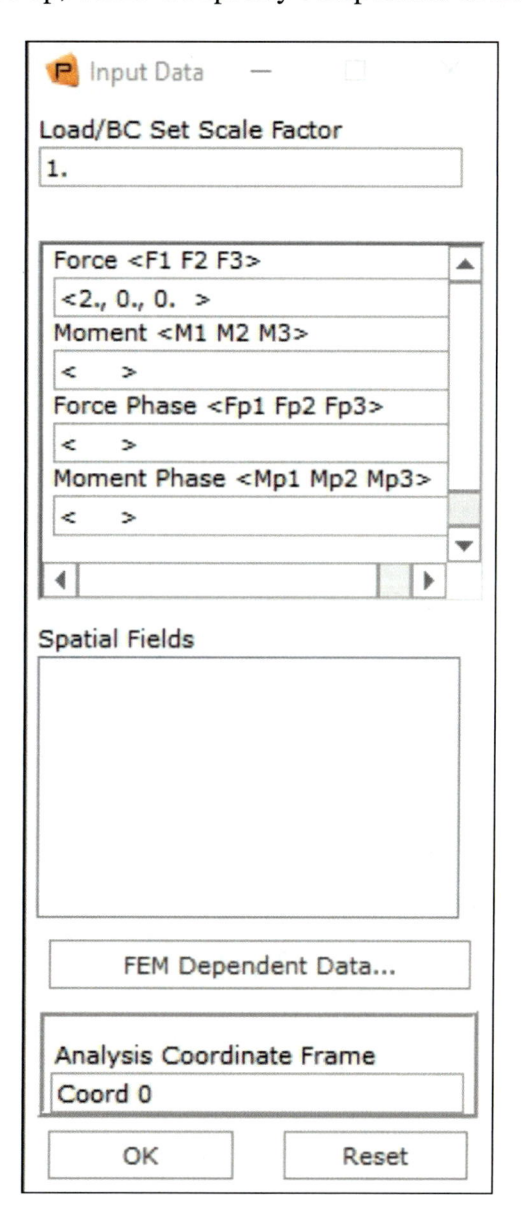

Click **OK** in the **Input Data** panel.

In the **Load/Boundary Conditions** RHS Window, click **Select Application Region…**
The **Select Application Region** RHS Window shows up, where we specify the command
Select: FEM, click in the field **Select Nodes**, and click at the Node 3 in the display window. The name **Node 3** shows up in the **Select Nodes** field:

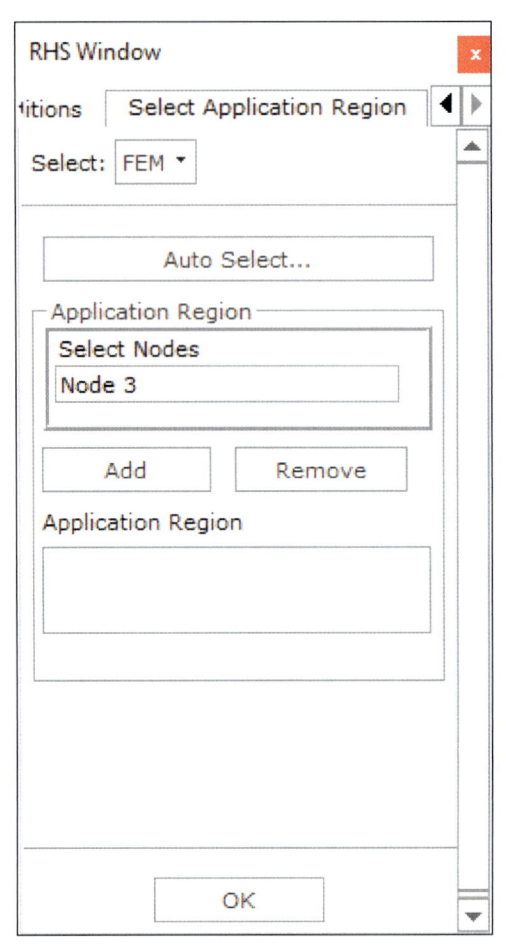

Click **Add** and **OK** in the **Select Application Region** RHS Window.

In the **Load/Boundary Conditions** RHS Window, click **Apply**. The name **Force** moves into the **Existing Sets** field:

and shows up in the **Model Browser**:

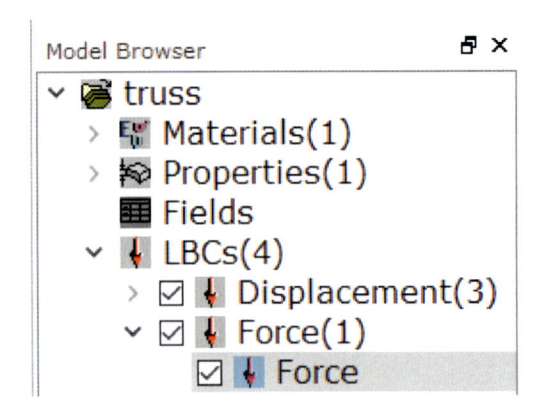

The force vector and its magnitude, **2.00**, show up in the display window:

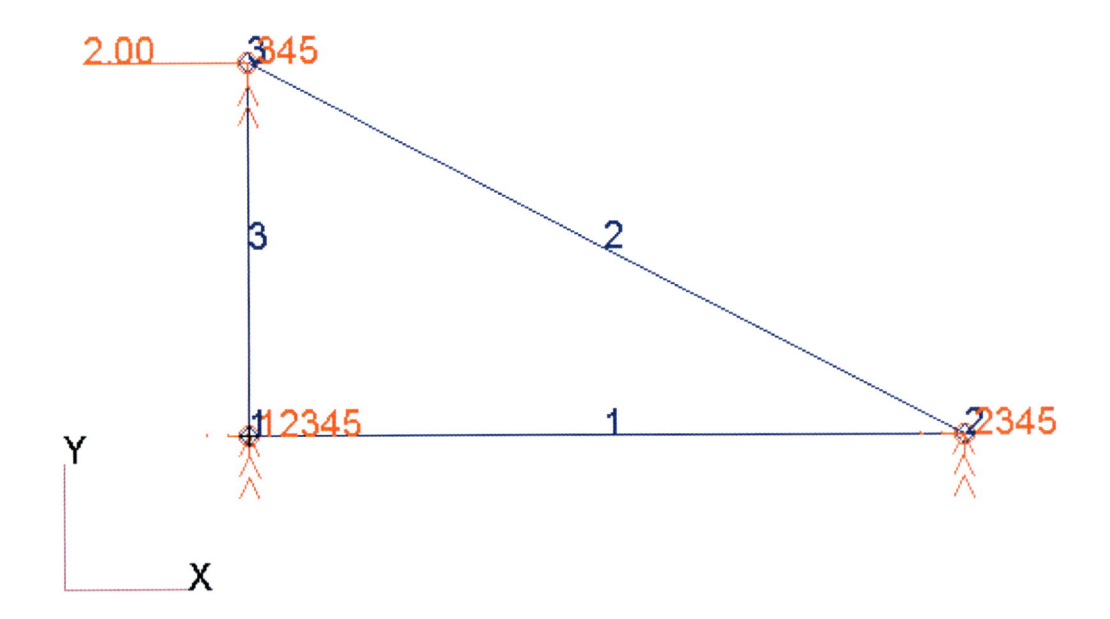

Close the **Load/Boundary Conditions** RHS Window.

2.7 Running Analysis

Open the **Analysis** application:

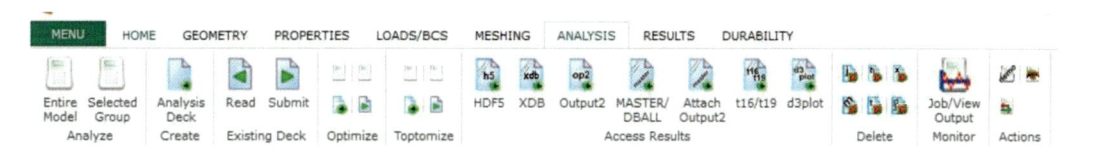

The **Analysis** RHS Window shows up, where we specify the following commands:

Click **Solution Type…**, the **Solution Type** RHS Window shows up, were we make sure that the **LINEAR STATIC Solution Type** is selected.

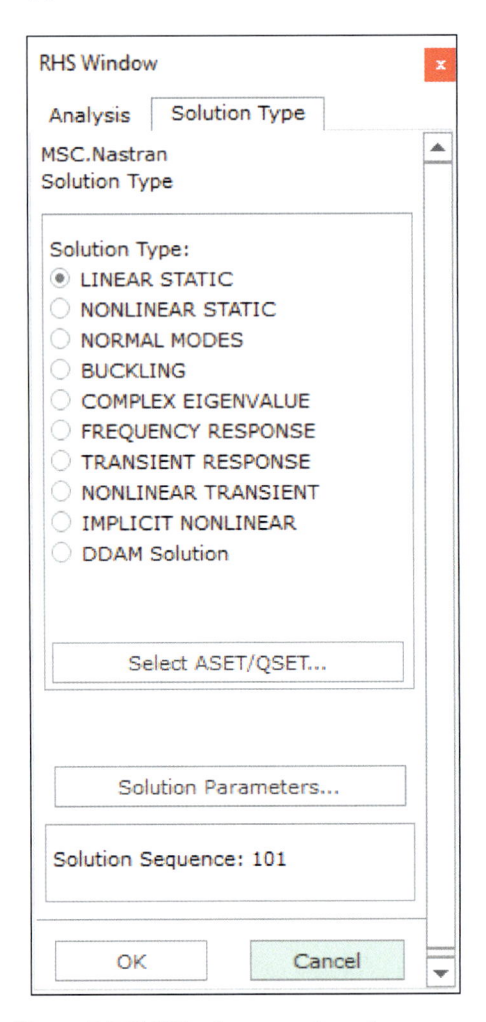

Click **Cancel** in the **Solution Type** RHS Window to close it.
In the **Analysis** RHS Window , Click **Subcases…**. The **Subcases** panel shows up, where we click **Output Requests…** The **Output Requests** panel shows up. In the **Select Results Type** field, select **Element Stresses**, **Constraint Forces**, and **Element Forces**.

The corresponding names of the requested output results move into the field **Output Requests**:

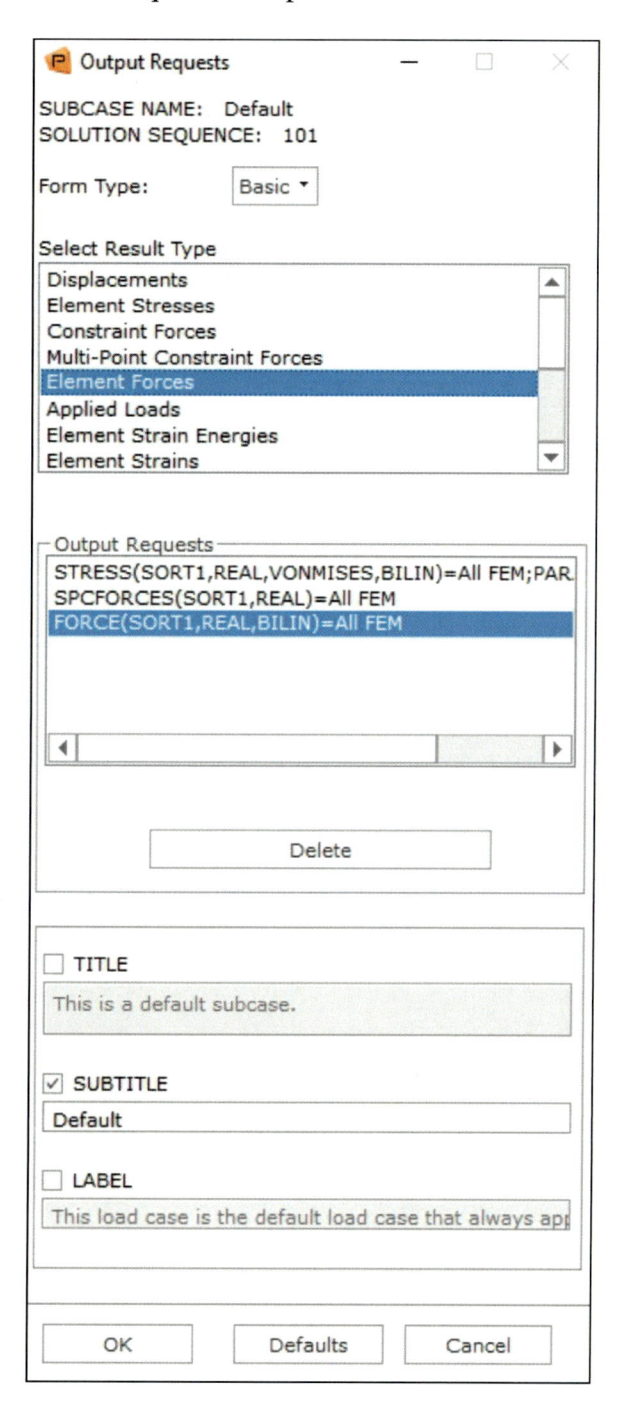

Click **OK** in the **Output Requests** panel. In the **Subcases** panel, click **Apply** and **Cancel**.

In **Analysis** RHS Window, click **Apply**. Analysis begins running. Completion of the analysis is indicated by creation of the file *truss.xdb*, containing the analysis results, and by the message "*MSC Nastran finished*" in the end of the file *truss.log*.

To import the analysis results into Patran, in the **Analysis** RHS Window, perform the following commands:

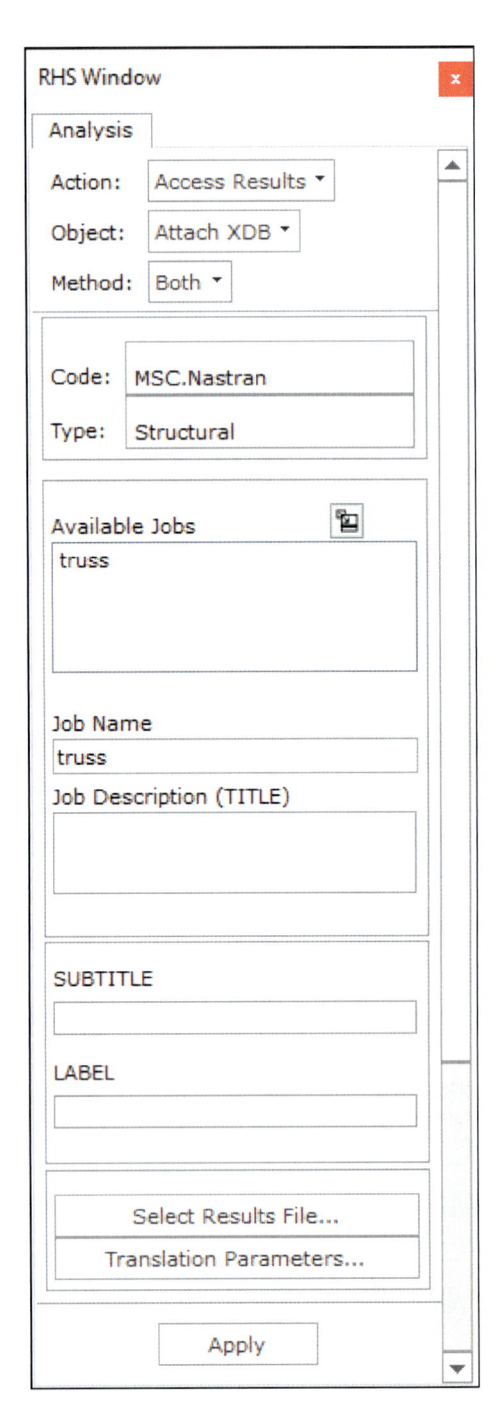

Click **Select Results File…** Select file *truss.xdb*. Click **OK**. Click **Apply** in the **Analysis** RHS Window.

Result Cases(1) shows up in the **Model Browser**:

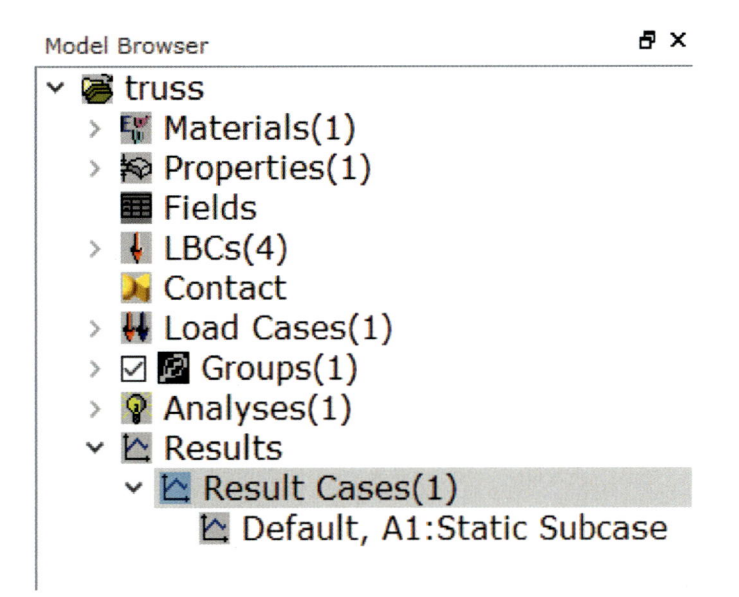

```
Model Browser
 v  truss
    >  Materials(1)
    >  Properties(1)
       Fields
    >  LBCs(4)
       Contact
    >  Load Cases(1)
    >  ☑ Groups(1)
    >  Analyses(1)
    v  Results
       v  Result Cases(1)
             Default, A1:Static Subcase
```

Close **Analysis** RHS Window.

2.8 Viewing results of analysis

2.8.1 Viewing internal forces in rods

Open the **RESULTS** application:

The **Results** RHS Windows shows up, where we select the following commands:

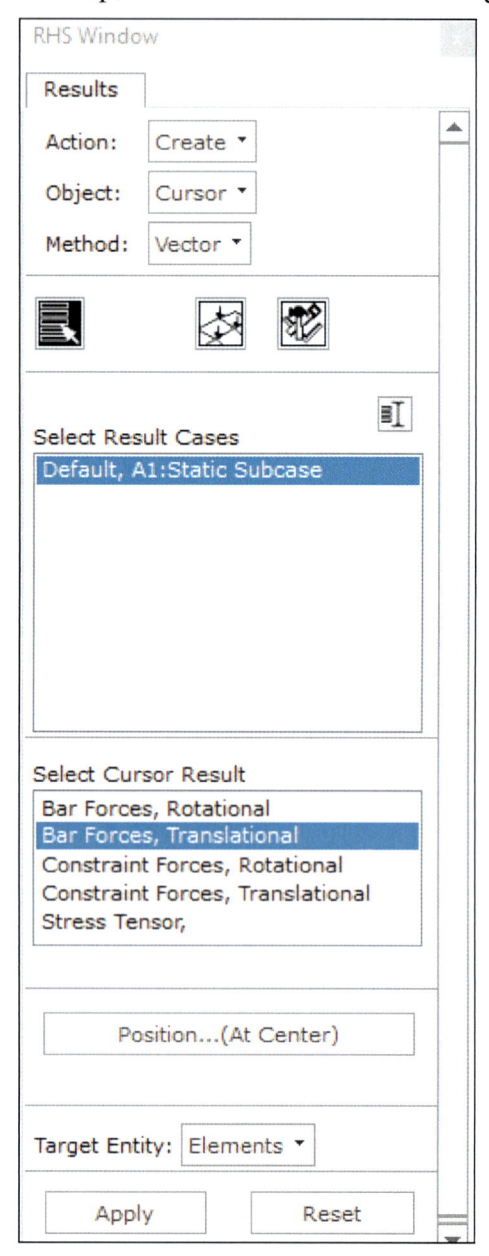

Click **Apply**.

The **Cursor Data** panel shows up:

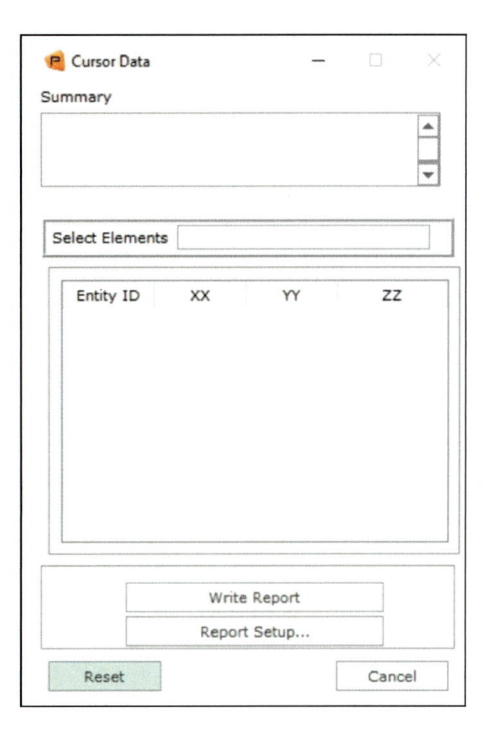

Click in the field **Select Elements**. Click at the element 1 (rod *AB*) in the display window. This produces the following results in the **Cursor Data** panel:

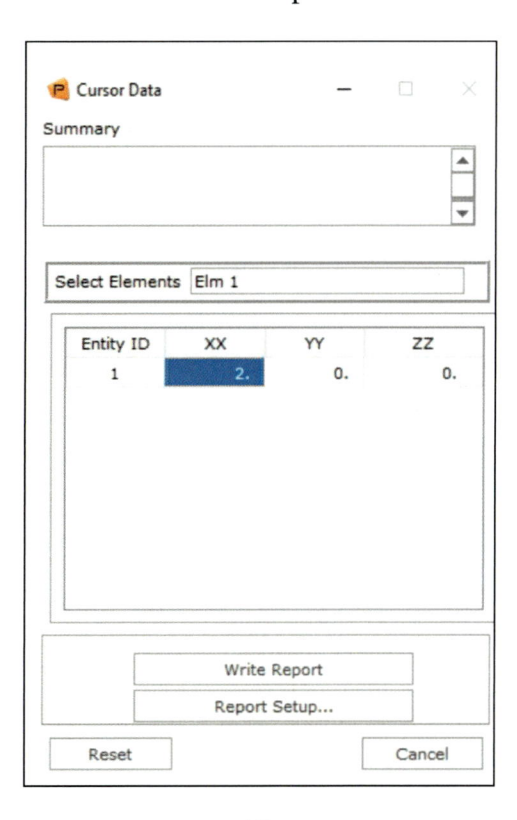

53

The value *2.* under *XX*, is the internal longitudinal force in the element 1 (rod *AB*), i.e. $N^{AB} = 2$, calculated analytically in the section 1 of the text.

Click in the field **Select Elements**. Click at the element 2 (rod *BC*) in the display window. This produces the following results in the **Cursor Data** panel:

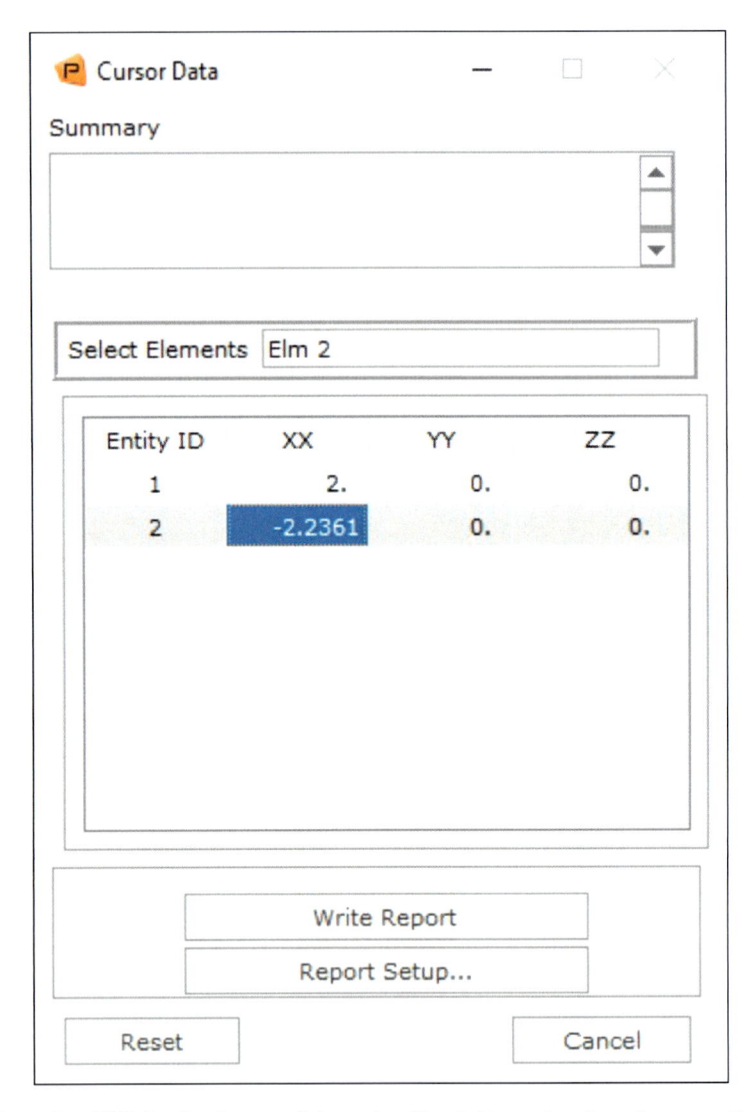

The value *-2.2361* under *XX*, is the internal longitudinal force in the element 2 (rod *BC*), i.e. $N^{BC} = -2.2361$, calculated analytically in the section 1 of the text. Such Nastran terminology (*XX*) for the internal force N^{BC} implies that the stress components in a rod are measured relatively to a local coordinate system, such that the local x-axis is parallel to the rod's axis.

Click in the field **Select Elements**. Click at the element 3 (rod AC) in the display window. This produces the following results in the **Cursor Data** panel:

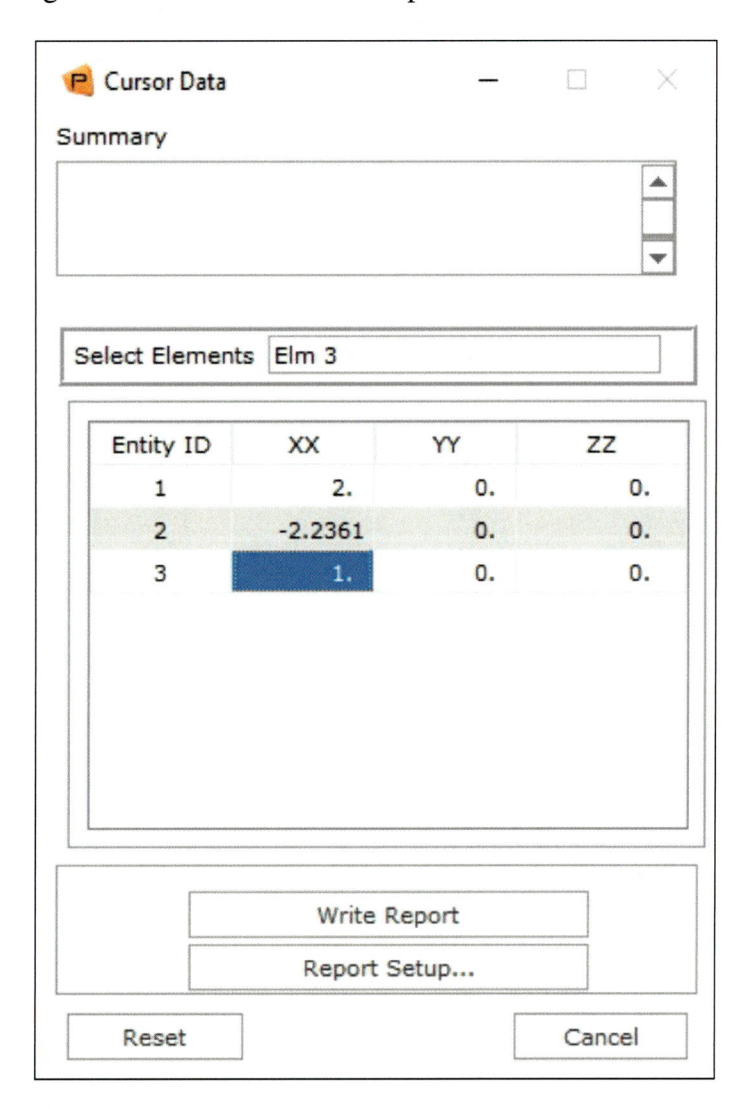

Entity ID	XX	YY	ZZ
1	2.	0.	0.
2	-2.2361	0.	0.
3	1.	0.	0.

The value *1.* under *XX*, is the internal longitudinal force in the element 3 (rod *AC*), i.e. $N^{AC} = 1.$, calculated analytically in the section 1 of the text. Such Nastran terminology (*XX*) for the internal force N^{AC} implies that the stress components in a rod are measured relatively to a local coordinate system, such that the local x-axis is parallel to the rod's axis.

The internal longitudinal forces in the rods are displayed also in the file "*truss.f06*":

FORCES IN ROD ELEMENTS (CROD)

ELEMENT ID.	AXIAL FORCE	TORQUE	ELEMENT ID.	AXIAL FORCE	TORQUE
1	2.000000E+00	0.0	2	-2.236068E+00	0.0
3	1.000000E+00	0.0			

2.8.2 Viewing components of stress tensor

To display components of the stress tensor in the rods, with respect to local coordinate systems such that the local x-axes are parallel to the rods, in the **Results** RHS Window, specify the following commands:

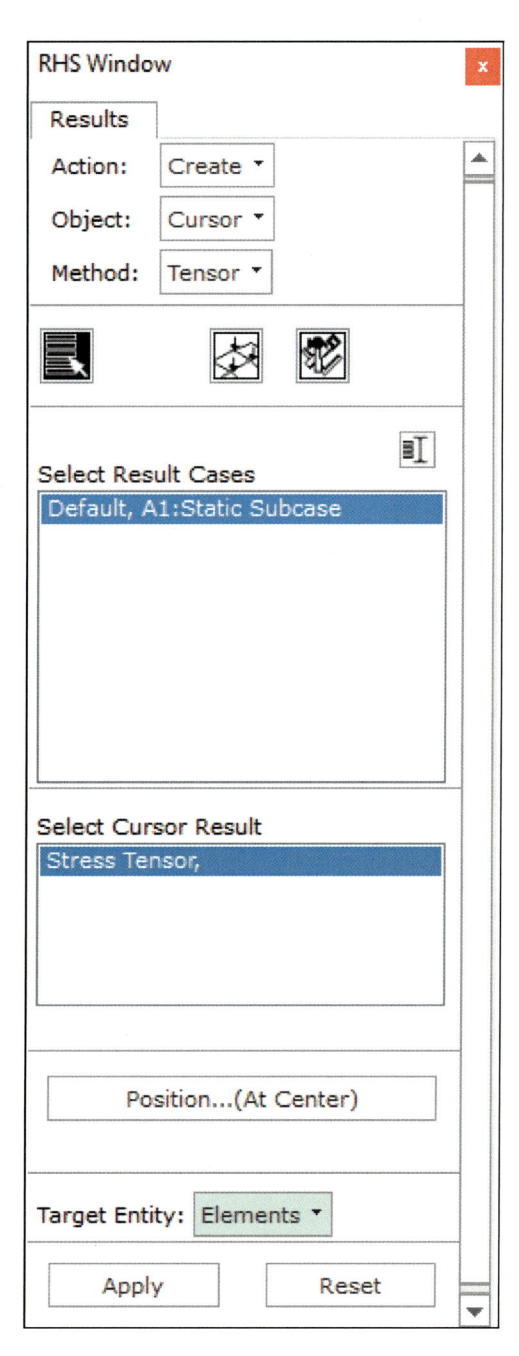

Then, performing the same operations as previously for displaying the internal forces in the rods, we receive

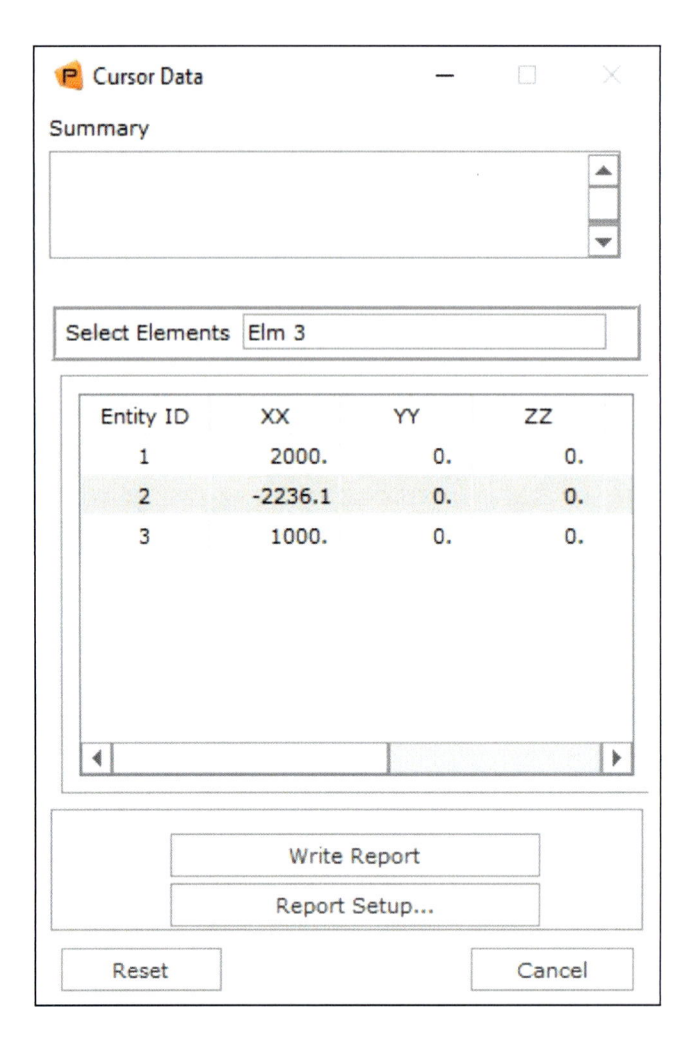

These results are the same as those obtained previously analytically.

The axial stresses are displayed also in the file "*truss.f06*", as shown below:

S T R E S S E S   I N   R O D   E L E M E N T S   (C R O D)

ELEMENT ID.	AXIAL STRESS	SAFETY MARGIN	TORSIONAL STRESS	SAFETY MARGIN	ELEMENT ID.	AXIAL STRESS
1	2.000000E+03	0.0			2	-2.236068E+03
3	9.999999E+02	0.0				

2.8.3 Viewing constraint forces

To display x-components of the constraint forces (relatively to the problem coordinate system, shown in the display window) at the joint *A* (Node 1) and the joint *B* (Node 2), in the **Results** RHS Window, specify the following commands:

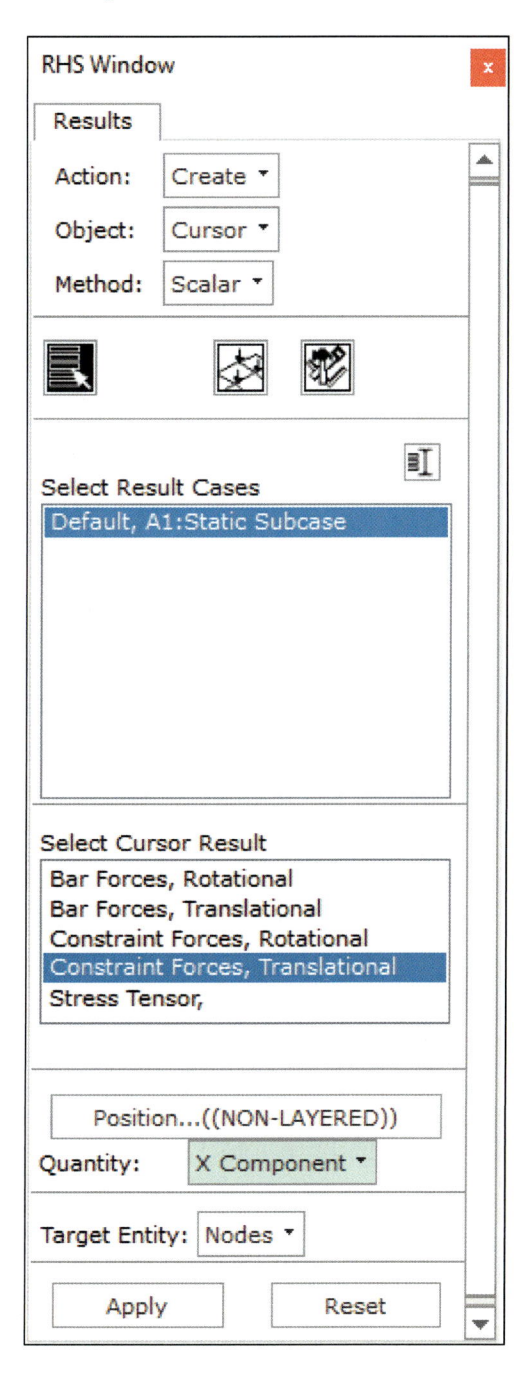

Click **Apply**.

The **Cursor Data** windows shows up, where we click in the **Select Nodes** field, and then click at the Node 1 (joint *A*) and the Node 2 (joint *B*) in the display window; the resulting values are displayed as shown below

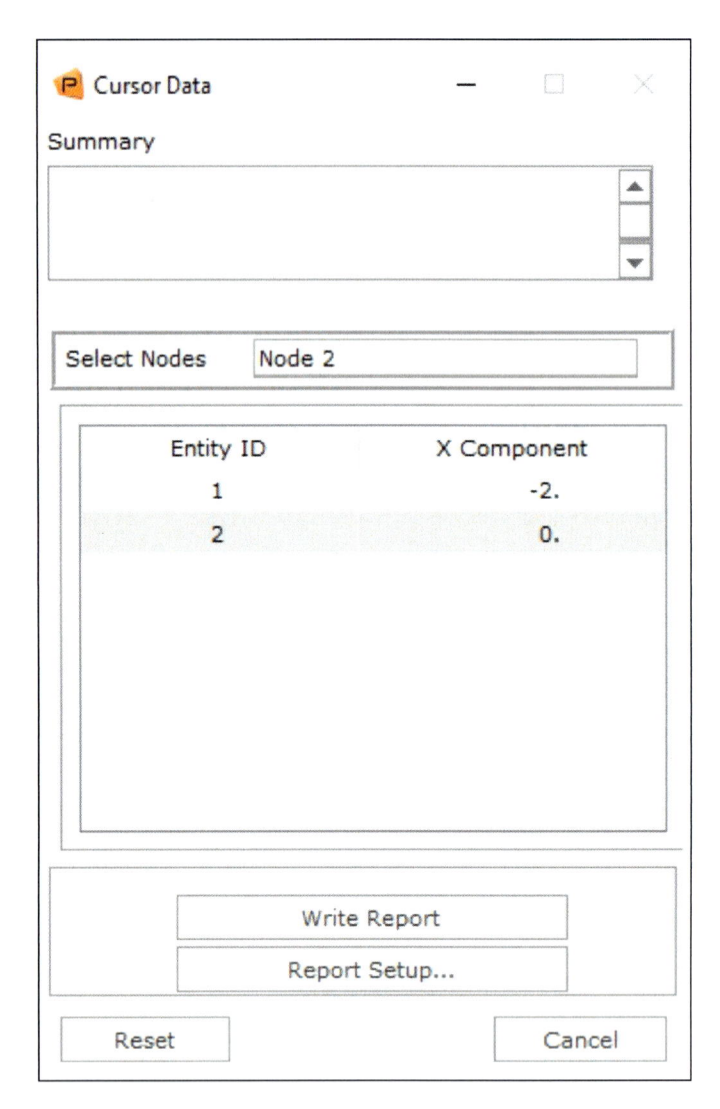

Entity ID	X Component
1	-2.
2	0.

Click **Cancel** in the **Cursor Data** panel to close it.

These results are the same as those obtained previously analytically: $R_x^A = -2$, $R_x^B = 0$.

To display y-components of the constraint forces (relatively to the problem coordinate system shown in the display window) at the joint A (Node 1) and the joint B (Node 2), we perform the similar operations. The resulting values are displayed as shown below

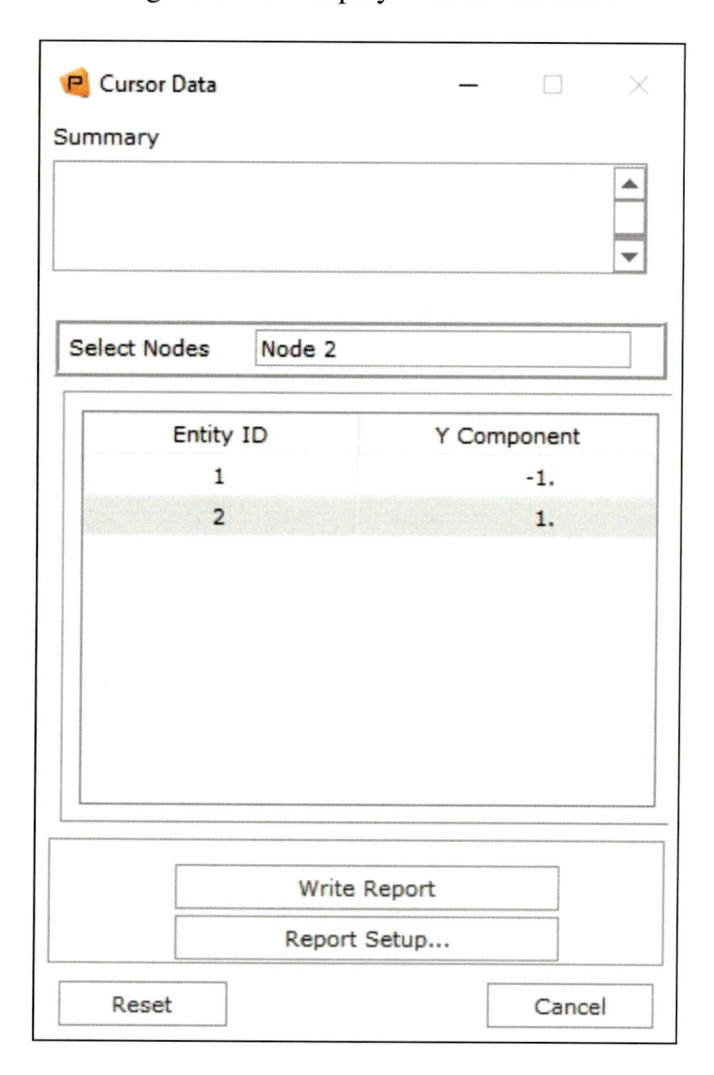

These results are the same as those obtained previously analytically: $R_y^A = -1$, $R_y^B = 1$.

The components of the reaction forces are displayed also in the file "*truss.f06*", as shown below:

FORCES OF SINGLE-POINT CONSTRAINT

POINT ID.	TYPE	T1	T2	T3
1	G	-2.000000E+00	-1.000000E+00	0.0
2	G	0.0	1.000000E+00	0.0

Made in the USA
Las Vegas, NV
11 March 2025